WELCOME TO
HOCKEY
LEGENDS

Lunar Press is a privately-run
publishing company that cares
greatly about its content's accuracy.

If you notice any inaccuracies or have
anything that you would like to
discuss in the book, then please email
us at
lunarpresspublishers@gmail.com.

Enjoy!

CONTENTS

FACE OFF

Ice hockey is pretty different from every other sport in the world. Okay, so there are goals, assists, overtime, buzzers, and many other things resembling football, basketball, and soccer. But hockey mixes grace and fierce power like nothing else. It is a one-off.

When people in Ireland and Britain first started playing hurling* and other stick-and-ball games in the 18th century, they never would have guessed that one form of their sport would become ice hockey. It wasn't until these Irish and British people emigrated to North America that ice hockey was born.

These people had witnessed harsh winters before, but nothing like the frozen lakes and biting cold of Canada and parts of America. With their hurling fields out of action, kids and adults alike started playing their favorite stick-and-ball games on the ice. When they realized they needed a flat "ball," the puck was invented. Everything fell into place once this new sport was mixed with ice skating!

Since then, ice hockey has grown and grown. Through legends such as Gordie Howe all the way up to Sidney Crosby and beyond, the NHL has become the most-watched hockey league on the planet. It has been brought to life in movies such as The Mighty Ducks and endless video games. How can we forget the hockey craze that took the world by storm in the eighties when Wayne Gretzky became a household name?

But Gretzky wasn't the only player to change the game. So many superstars have come along throughout the last couple of centuries and flipped the script. Bobby Orr finished his career with two Art Ross Trophies as the league's highest goal scorer, even though he was a defenseman! Jaromír Jagr has played 35 professional seasons and counting!

To list every Hall of Famer would have been too much. Even breaking the best players in NHL history down to 20 was nearly impossible. If we had tried to number them from 1 to 20, it would have been even harder, so we've just put them on the list in random order. You see, in most sports, deciding who is the greatest really is a matter of opinion, and hockey is no different.

For some people, it's all about Stanley Cups, but if we go by the number of team trophies a player has won, Wayne Gretzky and Ray Bourque would be way down the list. For others, deciding who is the best of all time goes by what they did for the game: those players who changed it for the better.

Whatever the case, we've tried to fit as many true legends into this book as possible. We hope that you not only learn a few things along the way but that you enjoy yourself too!

Can you decide who is the greatest of all time? There's only one way to find out...

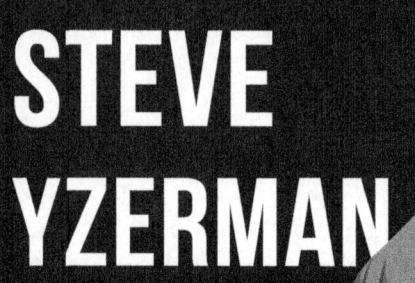

STEVE YZERMAN

THE CAPTAIN

TEAMS

DETROIT
RED WINGS

1983–2006

STANLEY CUPS
3

CAREER STATS

NHL FIRST TEAM ALL-STAR	1
BILL MASTERTON MEMORIAL TROPHY	1
CONN SMYTHE TROPHY	1
FRANK J. SELKE TROPHY	1
LESTER PATRICK TROPHY	1

GOALS	ASSISTS
692	1063

BIOGRAPHY

BORN	MAY 9, 1965
NATIONALITY	CANADIAN
POSITION(S)	CENTRE
SHOT	RIGHT
RETIRED	2006

As the longest-serving captain in NHL history, Steve Yzerman deserves his place on any greatest list. But he was never the type of captain who screamed and shouted on the ice. He led by example, spurring his teammates on with his passion and skill. Known for his graceful skating, Steve was an unselfish player who often gave up personal glory for the sake of the team.

In his time as a pro player, he won three Stanley Cups, a Canada Cup, and gold at the Winter Olympics with his beloved Canada. He is a true legend of the game.

Born in Cranbrook, British Columbia, Canada, on May 9, 1965, Stephen Yzerman loved hockey from the moment he could skate. As a kid (and even at the start of his NHL career), he played as an out-and-out center. That would change later in his career, but we will get to that soon! When he starred at the famous Quebec International Pee-Wee Hockey Tournament (QIPHT) as a kid, people already sensed that he would make it in the NHL. He was that good!

The QIPHT has produced a huge number of future NHL stars over the years, many of whom you will be hearing about in this book. Steve was one of the greatest to come through!

Steve attended Bell High School, where he played for the school's team. He was also a big player for his local

Nepean Raiders team. His performances for the Raiders got him spotted by the Peterborough Petes of the Ontario Hockey League (OHL), who signed him up soon after seeing him play.

After a year with the Raiders and then three with the Petes, Steve felt he was ready for the NHL. Surprisingly, a lot of teams overlooked him. The Detroit Red Wings' general manager, Jim Devellano, didn't even want to sign him. Devellano felt the franchise would be "settling" if they drafted Yzerman. The Red Wings had originally wanted to sign Pat LaFontaine.

In the end, they had to go for Steve, and Red Wings fans saw the 1983 NHL Entry Draft as a bit of a disaster. That soon changed, though, but Steve had to work hard to show everyone what he was made of. In fact, Devellano wanted to send Steve back to the Petes for a season as he didn't feel the kid was ready. It took one training camp for Devellano to change his mind, and Steve Yzerman would go on to play for the Red Wings for his whole career!

Through hard work and his natural talents, Steve's career took off like a bullet. In his rookie season, he recorded 39 goals and 48 assists, bringing his total points to 87. He finished second in the Calder Memorial Trophy (the award for the best rookie in the league) voting, and he became the youngest player in an NHL All-Star Game. He was just 18!

The 1985–86 season was when Steve really blew up. Following the departure of Red Wings' captain Danny Gare, Steve was given the role in his place. He was still a youngster, but his determination and skills were undeniable. Steve took on the responsibility like a fish to water, becoming the youngest captain in the franchise's history.

He kept shattering records. The following year, Steve registered his first 50-goal season when he scored against the Buffalo Sabres. He would have finished the year with more goals, but a serious injury later in the game meant he missed the rest of the season. But Steve and his team had done enough earlier in the season, and the Red Wings won their first division title in 23 years!

He kept improving, and the 1988–89 season saw Steve destroy his previous scoring record. He racked up 65 goals and 90 assists for a total of 155 points! He came third in the scoring chart and only behind Mario Lemieux and Wayne Gretzky, two legends we will cover later in this book. Steve finished the season with the Lester B. Pearson Award (now called the Ted Lindsay Award) for the most outstanding regular-season player.

Despite Steve's standout performances and the steady improvement of the Red Wings on the ice, success as a team seemed always to be a step too far. Things seemed to be getting worse when Scotty Bowman took over as head coach in 1993. He instantly clashed with Steve, claiming his captain didn't do enough defensively. Steve didn't like Scotty too much either and believed that his tactics were too rigid.

It got so bad that Steve came close to being traded to the Ottawa Senators. Thankfully for the Red Wings, the coach and player worked things out, and after a while, Steve improved under Scotty's guidance. Steve knuckled down and took some of his coach's advice on board, gradually becoming one of the best defensive forwards the league has ever seen.

With the two men working together, the Red Wings kept improving. They reached their first Stanley Cup Finals since 1966 (Steve's first-ever), where they came up against heavy underdogs, the New Jersey Devils. Shockingly, the Devils swept the Red Wings, inflicting a humiliating 4–0 series loss.

Instead of sulking, Steve and the Red Wings started the following season on fire. They recorded a then-record 62-win regular season, reaching the playoffs as one of the favorites. In a classic game against the St. Louis Blues, Steve stole the puck off Wayne Gretzky and hit a slap shot from the blue line to score what is considered his greatest goal. Unfortunately, the Red Wings buckled under the pressure again, losing the Western Conference Finals in six games to the Colorado Avalanche.

Detroit had been heavy favorites in both of those Finals, and the team was starting to get a reputation of one that choked on the big occasions. The Red Wings put this rumor to rest when they won the Stanley Cup in 1997 and then retained it the following year. They won it again in 2001–02, giving Steve his third and final Stanley Cup!

He retired in 2006 and has worked as the Red Wings' general manager as well as several other roles through the years. Steve's passion for his beloved Red Wings will always remain. He played his whole career there, but who knows how things would have turned out for Detroit if Jim Devellano had not drafted one of the NHL's greatest-ever players!

GORDIE HOWE

MR. HOCKEY

TEAMS

DETROIT RED WINGS

1946–1971

HOUSTON AEROS

1973–1977

HARTFORD WHALERS

1979–1980

STANLEY CUPS
4

CAREER STATS

ART ROSS TROPHY	6
HART MEMORIAL TROPHY	6
NHL FIRST ALL-STAR TEAM	12
LESTER PATRICK TROPHY	1
AVCO WORLD TROPHY	2

GOALS	ASSISTS
801	1049

BIOGRAPHY

BORN	MARCH 31, 1928
NATIONALITY	CANADIAN
POSITION(S)	RIGHT WING
SHOT	RIGHT (SOMETIMES LEFT)
RETIRED	1980

Is Gordie Howe the greatest of all time? Wayne Gretzky fans would probably disagree. Bobby Orr supporters might have something to say too! But for the Red Wings fans who saw Gordie Howe play throughout the 1950s and '60s, there hasn't been any better than Mr. Hockey.

Things didn't start off well for young Gordie. Life was tough. Born on March 31, 1928, in a farmhouse in Floral, Saskatchewan, Gordon Howe would know nothing but hard times in his early years. In fact, his family was forced to sell the farmhouse he was born in only nine days after his birth. A move to Saskatoon followed, where his father had to take a low-paying job as a laborer.

This was during the Great Depression when millions of people across North America were going hungry. Jobs were extremely hard to find, and for the few lucky people who found one, the pay was terrible. As a kid, Gordie had to go to work with his father to try to earn the family some extra money. In what little spare time he had, he played hockey.

He was eight when he first picked up a stick. At the time, hockey sticks were straight and not curved like today, and Gordie quickly discovered that he was ambidextrous. This means he could use his left hand as well as his right. It was a big advantage for him, as he could shoot from either side, an ability that helped him bamboozle* his opponents!

Gordie's childhood wasn't helped by the fact that he was dyslexic. We have to remember that this was in the 1930s, and people weren't as educated on such issues as they are now. Kids who struggled to read due to their dyslexia were called "dumb" and "stupid." It made his school years rough, but Gordie found an escape in sports.

His ability on the ice was obvious, and his body was growing fast. So fast, in fact, that his doctors thought he might have a calcium deficiency. They encouraged him to work out—mostly chin-ups—so his muscles could catch up with his bones. The result was that Gordie was six feet tall and built like a train by the time he was 14!

Gordie left school around this time as he had to work with his father to help pay the bills. After a couple of years of laboring, at the age of 16, he left Saskatoon to pursue his dream of being a professional hockey player.

It wasn't long before scouts from all the major franchises were sniffing around. The New York Rangers had tried to sign him when he was 15, but Gordie turned them down, feeling that he wasn't quite ready. In the end, he chose the Red Wings, and the rest, as they say, is history! Gordie Howe would go on to become an inspiration to millions of kids who wanted to be just like him.

Gordie was first moved to the Omaha Knights, one of

the Red Wings' affiliates* and a minor team in the United States Hockey League (USHL). At just 17, he scored 48 points in just 51 games. He was ready for the NHL.

He made his Red Wings debut at 18, playing in the right-wing position that he would soon make his own. He scored, instantly becoming a fan favorite. Gordie's rise was rapid, and the following season saw him being offered the number 9 jersey. He took on the responsibility, and soon, the number would be forever associated with Mr. Hockey.

Early in his career, Gordie became known for getting in fights as much as for his heroics with a puck. Pretty soon, the term "Gordie Howe Hat Trick" was born, which means a player scores a goal, an assist, and gets in a fight in a single game! The term is still used today.

The 1950s were immense for Gordie and the Red Wings. He led the league in scoring from 1950 through to 1954. There was a gap in '55, but Gordie again led the charts the following season. In that time, the Red Wings won four Stanley Cups. Gordie's form rarely, if ever, dropped, and he was still bossing it into the early 1960s and beyond.

But time catches up with everyone. After a while, his performances began to drop. With Gordie having less of an impact, the Red Wings' standards also suffered. Still, he managed to record his first and only 100-plus point season (1968–69) at the age of 40. He played on for two more years with the Red Wings, finally bringing his 25-year career in Detroit to an end in 1971.

But he wasn't done there! The newly formed World Hockey Association* had just begun, and with it came a lot of mega-contracts as the new league tried to pry the NHL's biggest stars away. Gordie was possibly the biggest name, and he was offered a lot of money to jump ship. He signed for the Houston Aeros, where he lined up on the ice alongside his two sons, Mark and Marty!

In his two years in Houston, he led the team to consecutive* titles, winning the MVP along the way. He was 46 when he won it! Gordie was such a legend even then that the league instantly renamed the MVP trophy the Gordie Howe Trophy!

As if all of that wasn't impressive enough, Gordie made a shock return to the NHL in his early fifties. At 52, he signed for the Hartford Whalers before the 1979–80 season. And he didn't just sign there to play the odd game. Gordie played in all 80 games that season, helping the Whalers to the playoffs and becoming the oldest player in history to appear in an NHL game.

He finished the season being picked for the All-Star Game, meaning he played in at least one All-Star Game in five separate decades! Yep, you read that correctly—decades!

After finally retiring, he settled down with his wife, Colleen, who had been his childhood sweetheart. Later in life, Colleen would be diagnosed with an incurable neurological disease* that eventually took her life. Gordie spent his remaining years raising millions for charity, mostly those that deal with such diseases.

He died in 2016, having been taken by the very disease he worked so hard to save others from. Gordie Howe will always be remembered as one of the best, and for the Red Wings fans who saw him play in the fifties and sixties, he is simply the greatest ever to take to the ice.

MIKE BOSSY

TEAMS

NEW YORK ISLANDERS

1977–1987

CAREER STATS

FIRST ALL-STAR TEAM	5
CALDER MEMORIAL TROPHY	1
CONN SMYTHE TROPHY	1
LADY BYNG MEMORIAL TROPHY	3
ALL-STAR GAME	7

STANLEY CUPS	GOALS	ASSISTS
4	573	553

BIOGRAPHY

BORN	JANUARY 22, 1957
NATIONALITY	CANADIAN
POSITION(S)	RIGHT WING
SHOT	RIGHT
RETIRED	1988

If Mike Bossy had remained injury-free throughout his short career, he would surely have managed more than nine full seasons. Unfortunately, that was all his health allowed. It's scary to imagine how many points he would have racked up if he'd played longer.

In those nine seasons he played, he scored 50 goals or more in every one of them, a record that has only been equaled by Wayne Gretzky and Alexander Ovechkin! Bossy was forced to retire at just 30, but he had already chalked up a staggering 1,126 points!

Michael Dean Bossy was born in the Ahuntsic-Cartierville area of Montreal on January 22, 1957. He was the fifth of ten kids, and with such a large family and little money, things were tough. The apartment the family shared was often cramped, but it meant that the Bossy boys and girls spent a lot of time outside playing. One of their favorite games was ice hockey!

When Mike was young, his father built a mini rink in the apartment block's backyard, meaning that when the outside lights were on, the kids could still practice at night. Mike took full advantage, regularly playing until his bedtime. He loved the game, and this passion could be seen years later in his pro career. He played like every game was his last!

Unfortunately, the injury problems that would affect

him throughout his short career began when he was just 12. To make matters worse, it didn't even happen on the ice! Mike broke his kneecap, an injury that rarely heals fully, competing in the long jump. Mike struggled with his knee until the day he retired.

Like so many stars in this book, Mike's youth career really took off at the Quebec International Pee-Wee Hockey Tournament, where he played for Laval National. In five seasons, he scored 309 goals. Shockingly, he was overlooked by most of the biggest teams in the NHL draft, as they felt he was too weak defensively. With a total of 532 points at youth level (which is still a record!), they maybe shouldn't have been too concerned with his defensive abilities!

In the end, the New York Islanders took a chance on him, a decision that would be one of the best the franchise had ever made. He was chosen in the 15th round of the draft after being passed over by everyone else. Bossy and the Islanders were made for each other.

Despite some people's fears that he wasn't cut out for the NHL, Bossy hit the ground running. He scored on his debut (a 3–2 loss to the Buffalo Sabres), and he pretty much continued scoring for the rest of his career! Still, he had a while to go before he would become an all-time legend, but Mike Bossy was never afraid of a little hard work.

He quickly edged regular right-winger Billy Harris out of the team, forming a destructive partnership with Bryan Trottier and Clark Gillies that became known as the Trio Grande. These three future Hall of Famers would soon help lead the Islanders to four Stanley

Cups in a row, which remain the only four the franchise has ever won.

As a winger, Mike Bossy was extremely strong in all departments. He was quick, graceful, powerful, and had a great shot. All these traits were seen in his rookie season, and he finished the year with the Calder Memorial Trophy. In that 1977–78 season, he registered 53 goals (including his first hat trick), a record that stood until 1993. It's safe to say that all the teams that overlooked him were kicking themselves!

One of that season's high points was another hat trick he scored, this time against rivals the New York Rangers (a team that passed on him twice in the draft). The Trio Grande combined for a total of 17 points in a 9–4 win! It was one of the greatest frontline performances of all time.

His rapid rise continued, and just a year later, he scored his 100th goal. It took Mike a mere 129 games to hit this milestone*.

By the 1979–80 season, Mike Bossy was one of the biggest stars in the NHL. Unfortunately for him (and every other player in the league!), his best years came in the 1980s, a decade Wayne Gretzky dominated in terms of individual awards. The Hart Memorial Trophy, the award given at the end of each year for the league's MVP, was won by Gretzky every year from 1980 to 1987. That was the period of the Islanders' dynasty, so Mike and his teammates might have felt a little peeved that they were constantly overlooked for MVP.

In his first two seasons, the Islanders won the division championship, but they couldn't make that final step and win their first Stanley Cup. It was clear that something amazing was being built, though. By the 1979–80 season, the team was expected to challenge again, and they did, but it didn't start well. They won only 6 of their opening 21 games, recording their worst start in over six years. They picked things up in the second half of the season and managed to finish second.

This time, when they reached the Stanley Cup Finals, they completed the job, beating the Philadelphia Flyers 4–2 over six games. It was a massive moment and one that was made even better by the news that Bossy had signed a new long-term contract. Along with his Trio Grande sidekicks, the Islanders knew they would have possibly the best front line in the NHL for the next few years.

Three more Stanley Cups followed, one after the other, creating one of the nine official dynasties in NHL history*.

Bossy's injuries continued to pile up. He played at a time when there was little to no protection for attacking players, and defenders took full advantage. In fact, Mike was one of the most outspoken players when it came to bringing in new rules to protect players. A lot of the newer rules we have today are down to his hard work off the ice.

In the build-up to his tenth season, Mike felt a dull pain in his back. He played through the pain, but it was getting worse with each game. At the end of the season, he saw his doctor, who told him two of the discs in his lower back were basically destroyed. He was then informed that he would have to retire. There was nothing that could be done to fix it.

Heartbroken, Mike Bossy was forced to end his short but extremely successful career. He did so with an unbelievable 573 goals and 553 assists in just 752 games. In the 129 playoff games he played, he scored 85 goals and 75 assists. His records are staggering, and the work he did to try and make the game safer should always be appreciated.

Sadly, Mike passed away in 2022 at just 65, but he will always be remembered as the star of that New York Islanders dynasty. When every other team overlooked him, the Islanders took a chance. If they hadn't, would they even have won one Stanley Cup? Probably not.

NICKLAS LIDSTRÖM

THE PERFECT HUMAN

TEAMS

VÄSTERÅS IK

1987–1991

DETROIT
RED WINGS

1991–2012

STANLEY CUPS
4

CAREER STATS

NHL FIRST ALL-STAR TEAM	10
NORRIS TROPHY	7
CONN SMYTHE TROPHY	1
OLYMPIC GOLD MEDAL	1
WORLD CHAMPIONSHIP	1
VIKING AWARD	2

GOALS	ASSISTS
264	878

BIOGRAPHY

BORN	**28 APRIL 1970**
NATIONALITY	**SWEDISH**
POSITION(S)	**DEFENCE**
SHOT	**LEFT**
RETIRED	**2012**

Now we have our first non-Canadian on the list and one of the greatest European players in the history of the NHL. Nicklas Lidstrom was a defenseman who spent 20 years playing for the Detroit Red Wings before eventually becoming the franchise's vice president. In those two decades Nicklas played for the Red Wings, they never failed to reach the playoffs! He also played alongside the first player covered in this book, Steve Yzerman.

Nicklas Lidstrom was born in Krylbo, Sweden on April 28, 1970. He grew up idolizing Borje Salming, a fellow Swede and defenseman who also played for the Red Wings for a season after a successful 16-year career with the Maple Leafs. Nicklas played hockey from the moment he could hold a stick, performing well for his school team, where Skogsbo SK spotted him.

Nicklas was a big lad, and he continued to fill out as he grew. Despite his size, he never lost his grace on the ice, and skating always seemed to come very naturally to him. Still, his brute strength always stood out the most, and after a time at Skogsbo SK, he moved to VIK Vasteras IK, a team in Sweden that always produced top players.

He spent three years at Vasteras, scoring 12 goals and 30 assists in 103 games before the 1989 NHL Entry Draft. Nicklas was drafted by the Red Wings 53rd overall, but he was held back for a couple of years so he could get used to the higher standard of hockey in America. By the time the 1991–92 season came around, Nicklas was ready.

But he had another milestone to take care of first. He led Sweden to gold at the 1991 International Ice Hockey Federation World Championships and then followed that up soon after by making his Red Wings debut! It didn't take him long to make his name.

Nicklas Lidstrom's rookie season was a huge success, both defensively and offensively. He finished the year with 60 points, which was massively impressive given how important he was in defense. He soon earned a reputation as a strong, reliable, and durable* defenseman, and Nicklas just missed out on first place in the voting for the Calder Memorial Trophy.

In his third season, Nicklas helped the Red Wings reach the Stanley Cup Finals, but they were swept by the New Jersey Devils. The team learned from that disappointment and came back again in 1997, and this time, it was them that swept their opponents! They beat the Philadelphia Flyers 4–0 in the series to win the franchise's first Stanley Cup in 42 years!

Alongside Steve Yzerman and several other future Hall of Famers, including Sergei Fedorov, Viacheslav Fetisov, and Brendan Shanahan, the Red Wings reignited some of the franchise's dominance of the 1950s. They played with an energetic style that had never really been seen before, and they followed up the 1997 Stanley Cup victory by winning it again the next year with yet another sweep, this time over the

Washington Capitals.

That second Stanley Cup year was particularly special for Nicklas, as he finished the season leading the points chart for defensemen. His constant improvement continued, and he won his first James Norris Memorial Trophy as the league's best defenseman in 2001.

The Red Wings continued to play some amazing stuff, but they had to wait until 2002 for their next Stanley Cup Finals appearance. This time, they faced the Carolina Hurricanes, playing in their first-ever finals. Under the captaincy of Yzerman and the defensive grit of Lidstrom, the Red Wings won 4–1, giving them their third Stanley Cup in six years.

Nicklas was awarded his second Norris Trophy in a row at the end of the season, and he added the Conn Smythe Trophy (playoff MVP) at the end of the playoffs too. He did it again the following season, winning his third Norris Trophy in a row!

One of his best years was 2006. Following Steve Yzerman's retirement, Nicklas was handed the captaincy. Along with this amazing honor, he also led Sweden to gold at that year's Winter Olympics. He helped the Red Wings to the Conference Finals, but they fell short, losing to the Edmonton Oilers.

Nicklas's time as captain was a success. In the 2007–08 season, the Red Wings finished with the best record in the league on their way to winning the Stanley Cup. It was Nicklas's fourth and final Stanley Cup victory, and he became the first captain of a Stanley Cup-winning team to be born and trained in Europe.

The Red Wings reached the Finals again the following season but lost a close series in seven games to the Pittsburgh Penguins. The team reached the playoffs every year until Nicklas's retirement in 2012. The year before this, he had been awarded his seventh Norris Trophy, leaving him only one behind the record-holder, the great Bobby Orr!

Nicklas Lidstrom has always kept the Detroit Red Wings close to his heart, and his loyalty was rewarded in 2022 when he was named the franchise's vice president. He has four sons, all of whom play hockey at a very high level, with two starring in the Swedish Division 1.

Having won four Stanley Cups, a World Championship, and Olympic gold, it is safe to say that Nicklas Lidstrom is a born winner. He was also one of the greatest defensemen ever to step onto the ice, and his leadership skills were essential to the Red Wings' success. He is a Detroit legend, which is the least to be expected of a man who earned the nickname "The Perfect Human"!

MARK MESSIER

THE MESSIAH

TEAMS

INDIANAPOLIS RACERS
1978
↓
CINCINNATI STINGERS
1979
↓
EDMONTON OILERS
1979–1991
↓
NEW YORK RANGERS
1991–1997
↓
VANCOUVER CANUCKS
1997–2000
↓
NEW YORK RANGERS
2000–2004

STANLEY CUPS
6

CAREER STATS

NHL FIRST ALL-STAR TEAM	4
CONN SMYTHE TROPHY	1
HART MEMORIAL TROPHY	2
LESTER PATRICK TROPHY	1
TED LINDSAY AWARD	2
CANADA CUP GOLD MEDAL	3

GOALS	ASSISTS
694	1193

BIOGRAPHY

BORN	JANUARY 18, 1961
NATIONALITY	CANADIAN
POSITION(S)	CENTRE / LEFT WING
SHOT	LEFT
RETIRED	2005

Moving on from one natural leader to another, we have Mark Messier, a player who proved his leadership qualities by becoming the only player in NHL history to captain two separate franchises to Stanley Cup victories. In his 25-year career, he managed to rack up 295 playoff points, the second-most ever, while playing in 1,756 regular season games, the third highest of all time! Along the way, he picked up six Stanley Cup trophies and earned the nickname "The Messiah," which pretty much speaks for itself!

Originally a left-winger, he had all of the attributes to play anywhere across the front line. Mark Messier was so much more than your average winger, as his switch to center soon after his NHL career began proved. At 6-foot-2 and strong, he could bodycheck his way to goal just as easily as glide his way there. In his early years, his style on the ice drew a lot of comparisons to Gordie Howe.

Mark was born in St. Albert, Alberta, to Mary Jean and Doug Messier. Doug was a former hockey star who played for the Edmonton Flyers and the Seattle Totems, among others. Mark's older brother Paul would also grow up to be a good player, and when they were young, Paul was the one most people presumed would make it to the top. Of course, Mark ended up being the Hall of Famer in the family, but Doug and Paul were fantastic on the ice too!

Although he was born in St. Albert, Mark spent most of his early childhood in Portland, Oregon. His father had signed for the Portland Buckaroos, a team in the Western Hockey League, so the family had to relocate. When his father retired from the game in 1969, the Messiers returned to their hometown.

Mark was brilliant from an early age, having spent most of his childhood practicing with his older brother and father. By his teens, he was surpassing all expectations. Even so, when he tried out for the Spruce Grove Mets (now the St. Albert Saints) at the age of 15, even his family thought he might be biting off more than he could chew. Although the Mets were a junior team, the cutoff point was 20, so most of the players in the league were adults.

Mark killed it at the tryouts and was offered a contract soon after. In his first season, he managed 66 points in just 55 games and was named captain the following year. He was only 16. In his first season as captain, he brought his total up to 74 points.

After a couple of years with the Mets, Mark had gathered a reputation as one of the most exciting prospects in the world. He spent a short time with the Indianapolis Racers of the World Hockey Association (WHA) just before it folded, before a slightly longer spell with the Cincinnati Stingers. Although his time in the WHA helped him to grow as a player, Mark always had his sights set on the NHL.

His chance came in the 1979 NHL Entry Draft when he had just turned 20. The Edmonton Oilers selected Mark in the third round, where he would team up with

Wayne Gretzky as part of one of the greatest teams in the history of the NHL.

Mark's rookie season wasn't the best. He had a lot of disciplinary issues, including one time when he missed a team flight. He was demoted to the Houston Apollos, the Oilers' affiliate team that played in the Central Hockey League (CHL), a minor league at the time. To keep himself out of trouble, Mark moved back in with his parents, knowing they would keep him in check.

But it wasn't just his bad discipline that was holding Mark back. His performances on the ice were below par too. He was highly respected for his competitiveness and leadership in the locker room, but his scoring was nothing special. That all changed in the 1984 playoffs when he was switched to center. The change was dramatic, and Mark soon became the player we all know and love.

He scored what is probably his most memorable goal in Game 3 of that year's Finals. With the Oilers losing to the reigning champions and Mike Bossy-led New York Islanders (who were looking to make it five in a row, remember!), Mark scored a goal following a superb end-to-end rush. It sparked an Oilers comeback, and they went on to win their first Stanley Cup and begin a famous dynasty.

Mark was awarded the Conn Smythe Trophy at the end of the season!

That Stanley Cup victory ended the Islanders' dynasty and began the era of the Oilers. They won it again in 1985, '87, '88, and '90. Mark was captain for the last of these victories, made even more impressive because the team did it without star player Wayne Gretzky, who had been traded to the Los Angeles Kings for the 1988–89 season. Messier topped off 1990 with the Hart Memorial Trophy as the league's MVP.

But things with the Oilers soon turned sour. After falling out with the hierarchy*, Mark was traded to the New York Rangers in a move that shocked the fans. He didn't waste any time feeling sorry for himself, and in his first season in New York, Mark helped the team to the best record in the league. Unfortunately, they were shocked by the Pittsburgh Penguins in the second round of the playoffs.

A poor 1992–93 season followed, but it was only a bump in the road. In Mark's third season with the Rangers, they again finished with the best record in the league. In an epic battle with the New Jersey Devils in the 1994 Eastern Conference Finals, Mark stunned reporters by guaranteeing the Rangers would be victorious, even though they had just gone 3–2 down in the series. The team won the next two games to set up a mouthwatering clash with the Vancouver Canucks in the Stanley Cup Finals.

Mark scored the winning goal in Game 7 in a double-overtime classic, leading the Rangers to a 4–3 series win to lift the franchise's first Stanley Cup in 54 years! It was Mark's sixth overall and his first with New York. It also made him the first man to captain two separate franchises to Stanley Cup glory!

His longevity* was one of Mark's strongest assets, and even into his mid-thirties, he was a force to be reckoned with. He recorded a 99-point season in 1995–96 at the age of 35. The following year, his old teammate Wayne Gretzky joined him at the Rangers. Much discussion in the media followed as to who would be named captain. Mark was told he would keep the captaincy, which only proves the huge respect held for the man.

As his career began to wind down, Mark still felt like he could play at the top. The Rangers disagreed, and at 36, he was traded to the Vancouver Canucks, who he had scored the winning goal against in Game 7 of the Stanley Cup a few years before! He played three years with the Canucks before New York realized their mistake and brought him back at the age of 40!

Mark was instantly handed the captaincy and went on to record a 67-point season despite his age. Two years later, he scored two goals in a game against the Dallas Stars to surpass the great Gordie Howe on the all-time points list (1,851). In his final game as a pro, Mark was applauded every single time he touched the puck and then received a standing ovation at the end. He retired at 43, and soon after, his jersey numbers at both the Oilers and the Rangers were retired.

Mark's son Lyon is also a former player who spent several seasons in the East Coast Hockey League (ECHL) and the Central Hockey League (CHL), meaning three generations of Messiers have played top-level hockey. Outside of the sport he loves, Mark Messier does a lot for charity. He is especially active in the New York Police and Fire Widows' and Children's Benefit Fund.

To play alongside a prime Wayne Gretzky on that 1980s Oilers team and still be considered a legend takes something special. Mark Messier not only achieved this, but he carved out his own path as a New York Rangers legend too. Some fans would even claim Mark was better than the Great One.

PATRICK ROY

SAINT PATRICK

TEAMS

MONTREAL CANADIENS

1984-1995

COLORADO AVALANCHE

1996-2003

STANLEY CUPS
4

CAREER STATS

NHL FIRST ALL-STAR TEAM	4
CALDER CUP	1
CONN SMYTHE TROPHY	3
VEZINA TROPHY	3
WILLIAM M. JENNINGS TROPHY	5
TRICO GOALTENDER AWARD	2

SO	GAA	SV%
66	2.54	.910

BIOGRAPHY

BORN	OCTOBER 5, 1965
NATIONALITY	CANADIAN
POSITION(S)	GOALTENDER
CAUGHT	LEFT
RETIRED	2003

It's very hard for a goaltender to earn the same kind of praise as an attacking player, as the goal scorers and assist kings usually make the headlines. So, when a goaltender gets called a legend, they must have been superb. Patrick Roy is a legend, and that's why he is on this list.

The man nicknamed the "King of Goaltenders" and "Saint Patrick" remains the only player to have won the Conn Smythe Trophy three times, and to make things even more special, he did it in three separate decades! Much like Mark Messier, the two franchises he played for retired his jersey. He is credited as the inventor of the "butterfly style" of goaltending, which is a style that is considered essential today.

Born in Quebec City on October 5, 1965, Patrick grew up in Cap-Rouge. Hockey was in his blood, and his younger brother also played professionally, clocking up 12 NHL games before switching to the minor league, where he spent most of his career. As a kid, Patrick wanted nothing more than to be a pro player. While all his friends wanted to be Phil Esposito or Gordie Howe, Patrick looked up to Jacques Plante, Al Rollins, and the other top goaltenders at the time.

His performances in the 1977 and '78 Quebec International Pee-Wee Hockey Tournaments brought him to the attention of NHL scouts, who kept an eye on his progress in the following years. Patrick also starred for his local team, Sainte-Foy Gouverneurs, before progressing to the Granby Bisons of the Quebec Major Junior Hockey League.

In his late teens, Patrick started playing pro hockey with the Sherbrooke Canadiens in the AHL, where he waited for his dream of playing in the NHL to become a reality. It happened in the 1984 NHL Entry Draft, but in a different way than he would have wanted. In fact, when Patrick was selected (51st overall) by the Montreal Canadiens, he thought things couldn't have worked out worse. He grew up a Quebec Nordiques fan, who are the archrivals of the Canadiens!

His loyalties soon changed, and the more he played for the Canadiens, the more he fell in love with the team and the fans.

Patrick only had to wait until February 1985 for his debut, when starting goaltender Doug Soetaert was injured in the third period. The young Patrick Roy played the last 20 minutes without conceding a goal, helping his team to the win. He had set himself some very high standards!

His attitude and top performances earned him his place as the starting goaltender for the following season when Steve Penney came off injured during a game in January. Patrick played 47 games during the regular season as the Canadiens reached the Stanley Cup Finals. The Canadiens stunned the Calgary Flames 4–1, with Patrick Roy being awarded the Conn Smythe Trophy as playoff MVP. He was only 20, making him the youngest-ever winner of the award.

His wonderful performances during the Stanley Cup triumph led to him being given the nickname "Saint Patrick," as the fans claimed that some of his goaltending had been nothing short of miraculous. If Patrick had felt any more sadness at having joined the rivals of his childhood team, it surely vanished after this!

If the love of his fans wasn't enough to sway his loyalty, the 1992–93 season was the clincher. Following a pretty average regular season, the Canadiens crawled into the playoffs after finishing third. They were drawn against the Nordiques in the first round, meaning Patrick would come up against his boyhood team. To make it even more interesting, the Nordiques claimed that their goaltender, Ron Hextall, was the best in the business!

The Nordiques' mind games seemed to have worked when Patrick had a bit of a stinker in the opening two games, giving the Nordiques a 2–0 lead in the series. Some of the local newspapers claimed that Patrick Roy had lost the "Battle of the Goalies." Instead of making him shrink, the added pressure drove Saint Patrick on, and he dragged his team to a 4–2 series win!

In a team that finished the season with no players in the top 20 scorers' chart, Patrick somehow led the Canadiens to a Stanley Cup victory. The team's lack of points in attack was overshadowed by their solid defense, which Patrick was the main part of. But things didn't stay rosy, and when head coach Jacques Demers was replaced by Patrick's ex-teammate (and old enemy) Mario Tremblay, Patrick's days at the Canadiens were numbered.

Soon after his appointment, Tremblay began pushing Patrick out the door. They almost got into a fistfight on a couple of occasions, and when Tremblay waited as long as possible to sub Patrick out during an embarrassing 11–1 defeat (the franchise's worst-ever result), Patrick took it personally. As he skated off the ice, he told the Canadiens' president, Ronald Corey, that he would never play for the team again. He was traded to the Colorado Avalanche four days later.

Patrick Roy had spent 11 beautiful years with the Canadiens, but it was time to move on. Many so-called experts believed his successful years were behind him, having moved on from a good Canadiens team, but they were wrong. In fact, the Canadiens have yet to win a Stanley Cup since Patrick left, while the man himself went on to win two more with the Avalanche!

The first of these victories came in his first season with his new team. It was the first time in the franchise's history that they reached the Finals, but the team they came up against—the Florida Panthers—were also newbies! Patrick Roy's previous experience at that level paid off, and he helped the Avalanche to a 4–0 sweep to lift the Stanley Cup!

If that 1996 Stanley Cup was a landslide, the 2001 Finals was an epic. The Avalanche, looking for their second Stanley Cup and Patrick's fourth, came up against the Jersey Red Devils. Following a superb Patrick Roy shutout in Game 1, the Red Devils hit back by winning Game 2. Game 3 went to the Avalanche, but the back-and-forth continued when Jersey took Game 4 and 5! With the Red Devils only needing one more victory, Patrick performed heroics in Game 6 with yet another shutout, and then followed this up by only conceding one goal in Game 7 to lead the Avalanche to a 4–3 series win!

He was awarded the Conn Smythe Trophy at the end (the third of his career) as he cemented himself as an Avalanche legend. When his number 33 jersey was retired by both Colorado and the Canadiens, Patrick Roy made a very solid claim to be considered the greatest goaltender in history.

Following his retirement in 2003, Patrick tried his hand at coaching, including a stint in charge of the Colorado Avalanche, whom he led to the playoffs in 2014. He does a lot of charity work, mostly for Ronald McDonald House, an organization that has helped millions of children lead a better life.

Was there ever a better goaltender than Patrick Roy? Well, that's a question only you can answer!

PHIL ESPOSITO

TRADER PHIL

TEAMS

CHICAGO BLACK HAWKS

1963–1967

BOSTON BRUINS

1967–1976

NEW YORK RANGERS

1976–1981

STANLEY CUPS
2

CAREER STATS

NHL FIRST ALL-STAR TEAM	6
ART ROSS TROPHY	5
HART MEMORIAL TROPHY	2
LESTER PATRICK TROPHY	1
TED LINDSAY AWARD	2
NHL ALL-STAR GAME	10

GOALS	ASSISTS
717	873

BIOGRAPHY

BORN	FEBRUARY 20, 1942
NATIONALITY	CANADIAN
POSITION(S)	CENTRE
SHOT	LEFT
RETIRED	1981

Phil Esposito has done it all in hockey. He's been a star player, a record-breaker, a coach, an executive, and an owner. He was the first player to register more than 100 points in a season, and then went on to do it five more times! Apart from starring for the Blackhawks, the Boston Bruins, and the New York Rangers, he is also the older brother of Hall of Fame goaltender Tony Esposito!

Born and raised in Sault Ste. Marie, Ontario, on February 2, 1942, Phil showed talent from an early age. After starring for his local and school teams, he was signed by the Chicago Blackhawks while still a teenager. But his talents were still raw, and he was assigned to their "B" team, the Sarnia Legionnaires, for a few years.

In his rookie season (1960–61) with the Legionnaires, Phil scored 47 goals and 61 assists for an average of 3.3 points per game. Despite this, he continued to be held back by the Blackhawks. They felt he needed to grow both physically and mentally if he were to compete in the NHL, which must have seemed odd to Phil when he was performing so well.

In one particular playoff game for the Legionnaires, he scored 12 points and won his team the Western Ontario final, but it still wasn't enough. By the time he made his NHL debut in 1964, Phil was 21 and champing at the bit*.

Pretty soon, Phil had become the team's starting center. The fans loved him, and he quickly showed that he was not only a heavy goal-scorer but also a top playmaker. In both of his first two seasons, he finished just off the top of the points chart. Despite his growing reputation, Phil was traded to the Boston Bruins in 1967, two years before his younger brother joined the Blackhawks!

Phil's move to the Bruins was seen as the most spectacular trade ever until that point, but he never let the pressure to perform get to him. If anything, it spurred him on. In his second season with the Bruins, Phil became the first player in NHL history to record a 100-point season and finished with 126. He failed to reach the same mark the following season but still managed 99.

After the disappointment of missing out on the 100 by a single point, Phil never looked back. He racked up 100-plus points in all of the next five seasons, claiming the Art Ross Trophy in 1969, '71, and '74. Between 1969 and 1975, he was the league's leading goal scorer and became one of the sport's first genuine global superstars.

Phil Esposito was so dangerous in front of the goal that fans started to bring signs to the stadium that read, JESUS SAVES, BUT ESPO SCORES ON THE REBOUND!

What makes all of Phil's achievements even more impressive is that he was never the quickest or even the most graceful player on the ice. What he had were unbelievable instincts and determination. He read the game differently from anyone else and seemed almost to sniff goal-scoring chances out. He kept the game simple, and it worked brilliantly.

During his time with the Bruins, Phil helped form one of the most dangerous front lines in the history of the NHL. Beside him at center was Bobby Orr, another legend who we will cover later in the book. On either side of them were Wayne Cashman and Ken Hodge, two Bruins all-time greats. When they all played together, there weren't many defenses that could handle them.

The Bruins won the Stanley Cup in 1970 and '72 while also recording first-place finishes in the league in 1971, '72, and '74. Surprisingly, the 1970–71 season that saw the Bruins top the league and Phil shatter the points record ended trophyless when the Bruins lost 4–3 to the Montreal Canadiens in the playoffs.

Phil's scoring record lasted until Wayne Gretzky came along and broke it in 1982. Phil, always known for his class and dignity, was in attendance that night and came onto the ice to present Gretzky with the game puck.

Following the highs of winning two Stanley Cups in three years, the relationship between Phil and the Bruins started to fail a little. He was told before the 1975–76 season that he wouldn't get as much playtime as he wanted due to his age. (He was 34.) Still feeling like he was at the top of his game, Phil moved on to the New York Rangers.

He got his playtime in New York, but some of his attacking sharpness had faded. But when he was really feeling it, there was still nobody like Phil Esposito, and he proved this at the age of 37 when he helped the Rangers to the 1979 Stanley Cup Finals. Unfortunately, it was a step too far for the team, and they were soundly beaten, but Phil had proved that he could still cut it at the top, as he'd promised.

Phil Esposito retired in 1981, second only to the great Gordie Howe in career goals and total points. With his skates hung up, Phil moved into coaching, becoming the New York Rangers general manager and head coach in 1986. While in charge, he became known as Trader Phil due to the number of players he signed and moved on! He stayed in the role for two seasons, leading the team to the division playoffs both years.

In 1990, he created and built the Tampa Bay Lightning franchise with his brother, Tony. Phil has worked in broadcasting, and he has even acted in several TV shows and commercials. He is a man of many talents, although his skills on the ice really made him stand out!

SIDNEY CROSBY

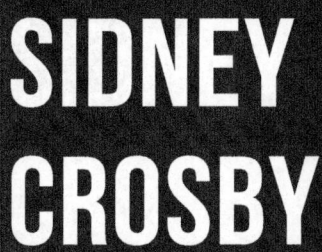

SID THE KID

TEAMS

PITTSBURGH PENGUINS

2005–2023*

STANLEY CUPS
3

CAREER STATS

NHL FIRST ALL-STAR TEAM	4
ART ROSS TROPHY	2
CONN SMYTHE TROPHY	2
HART MEMORIAL TROPHY	2
MARK MESSIER NHL LEADERSHIP AWARD	1
MAURICE RICHARD TROPHY	2

GOALS
565*

ASSISTS
964*

Sidney Crosby is still playing so his stats are accurate as of December 2023

BIOGRAPHY

BORN	**AUGUST 7, 1987**
NATIONALITY	**CANADIAN**
POSITION(S)	**CENTRE**
SHOT	**LEFT**
RETIRED	**STILL PLAYING**

In every sport, there are times when a young player comes along who everybody says is the next big thing. They are usually geniuses in their field, and the hype can reach fever pitch*. Quite often, though, the hype can become too much to live up to, and the kid crumbles under the pressure. How many potential superstars have we heard about who ended up never making it? It's not easy to make it in any sport, but cracking the NHL is one of the hardest of all.

One of the many youngsters who made a lot of waves as a kid was Sidney Crosby. When you are nicknamed "The Next One" before you've even played a game in the NHL, then the pressure is firmly on! But Sid the Kid more than lived up to the hype.

Sidney was born in Halifax, Nova Scotia on August 7, 1987. He grew up in nearby Cole Harbour, where his father played in the Quebec Major Junior Hockey League and won the President's Cup and the Memorial Cup two years before Sidney was born. That same year, Sidney's father was drafted by the Montreal Canadiens, but he never made an NHL appearance.

If his father had made it at the Canadiens, it would have been a dream for young Sidney. He loved the Canadiens growing up, and he idolized Steve Yzerman. Even as young as two, Sid could be found with a stick in his hand, shooting a puck into a net his father had set up in the basement. He never wanted to be anything other than an NHL star. He even learned to skate at the age of three!

But Sidney didn't just excel at sports. He was a straight-A student at Astral Drive Junior High School and a well-mannered, respectful kid. And there was always a lot of pressure on his young shoulders. Sidney was giving newspaper interviews as young as age seven as the hype around him grew, but he never let it go to his head. He always remained humble.

Throughout his teens, Sidney often turned down lucrative* offers to sign for pro teams, as he wanted to make sure he was ready. He performed so well in the Quebec Major Junior Hockey League (QMJHL) that he was awarded the Mike Bossy Trophy as the most outstanding prospect, and QMJHL even went so far as to retire his number 87 jersey in 2019!

Sidney stuck to his guns, and when the 2005 NHL Entry Draft came around, he felt he was ready. Every franchise wanted him, and he was considered the most sought-after prospect in NHL history. The Pittsburgh Penguins selected him first overall, and Sid the Kid was ready to tear it up in the NHL!

In his first home game—against the Boston Bruins—Sidney scored a goal and two assists and continued to impress as the season wore on. But things didn't always go smoothly. Head coach Ed Olczyk was fired midway through the season and was replaced by Michel Therrien. In a move that piled even more pressure on Sidney, Therrien named the 18-year-old star as alternative captain. The crowd didn't like it, as they thought it was far too soon for such responsibility.

The pressure on Sidney was immense, and it wasn't made any better when the Penguins finished with the worst record in the Eastern Conference. For a team expected to challenge for the Stanley Cup, this wasn't good enough. Sidney had a good personal record at the end of the year (39 goals and a franchise-record 63 assists), but he wanted the team to do well, not just himself.

The Penguins improved in Sidney's second season, and Sidney himself was killing it. He scored his first hat trick in an 8–2 demolition of the Philly Flyers and followed this up with his first six-point game a few weeks later. He ended the season with 36 goals and 84 assists in 79 games, becoming the first teenager to lead the NHL in scoring since Wayne Gretzky. (We'll get to The Great One soon, we promise!) Sidney also became the youngest-ever winner of the Art Ross Trophy at just 19.

When Sidney was made team captain at the end of his second season, nobody complained. Not this time. He was a bona fide superstar by now, and his teammates and fans loved him. At just 19 years, nine months, and 24 days, he became the youngest NHL captain in history.

The records continued to be broken, and he made it a rare hat trick of awards when he was given the Hart Memorial Trophy and the Lester B. Pearson Award to go with his Art Ross! He also became the youngest player to win the Lester B. and the youngest player to be picked for the All-Star Game!

Now, that's certainly living up to the hype!

Fearing that he might be tempted away, the Penguins tied Sidney down to a massive five-year contract before the 2007–08 season. They reached the Stanley Cup Finals at the end of the season but fell just short against the Nicklas Lidstrom-captained Red Wings. But the Penguins would be back the following year, amazingly coming up against the same opposition once more.

The two captains—Lidstrom and Crosby—already had massive respect for each other, but it grew even more after an epic 4–3 victory for the Penguins. In the process, Sidney became the youngest Stanley Cup-winning captain since 1895! He was only 21.

Following the highs of winning the biggest prize in hockey, Sidney faced his first real lows. A series of injuries would hamper him throughout his career. One of the worst was a concussion he suffered in January 2011 that was so bad it kept him out for nearly a year and almost forced him to retire.

A year before, Sidney had helped his native Canada win gold at the 2010 Winter Olympics, an achievement he ranks up there as one of his best. Despite his injury problems during this period, he also managed to squeeze in a 25-game points streak in the NHL, amassing 27 goals (including three hat tricks!) and 24 assists.

He signed a mammoth $104.4 million 12-year contract in 2011, but he had to wait until 2016 to lift his second Stanley Cup, which came at the end of an 85-point regular season. They beat the San Jose Sharks over six games, with Sidney being awarded the Conn Smythe Trophy. The Penguins retained their title the following year, beating the Nashville Predators over six games. Sidney picked up the Conn Smythe Trophy once again!

Sidney Crosby is still performing at the top level while this book is being written. He is the perfect example of how a professional player should conduct himself. He steers clear of social media and fame and just plays because he loves the sport. He is also the founder of several charities, including the Sidney Crosby Foundation, an organization that helps kids less fortunate.

What a player. What a man. What a pro.

JAROMÍR JÁGR

MARIO JR.

TEAMS

Team	Years
PITTSBURGH PENGUINS	1990–2001
WASHINGTON CAPITALS	2001–2004
NEW YORK RANGERS	2004–2008
PHILADELPHIA FLYERS	2011–2012
DALLAS STARS	2012–2013
BOSTON BRUINS	2013
NEW JERSEY DEVILS	2013–2015
FLORIDA PANTHERS	2015–2017
CALGARY FLAMES	2017–2018

CAREER STATS

Award	Count
NHL FIRST ALL-STAR TEAM	7
ART ROSS TROPHY	5
BILL MASTERTON MEMORIAL TROPHY	1
HART MEMORIAL TROPHY	1
TED LINDSAY AWARD	3

GOALS	ASSISTS	STANLEY CUPS
766	1155	2

BIOGRAPHY

BORN	15 FEBRUARY 1972
NATIONALITY	CZECH
POSITION(S)	RIGHT WING
SHOT	LEFT
RETIRED	STILL PLAYING

Not many players have been in the game for 35 seasons. And even fewer continue to compete at the age of 52! Well, Jaromír Jágr has done both of these things. The man from the Czech Republic was still playing when this book was written, and not just for any team. He was doing so for the team that he owns!

Jaromír Jágr was born in what was then called Czechoslovakia* on February 15, 1972. The man who would grow up to be an NHL star had it hard growing up. From an early age, he had to work on his family's farm in horrible conditions while also attending school in between. But Jaromír never complained, and he would later claim this upbringing toughened him up and gave him a solid work ethic.

He first started skating at the age of three, and it is said that he was graceful and powerful even then. By the time he was 15, Jaromír was competing against adults for his local team, and two years later, he made his debut for his national team! It was on this stage that NHL scouts spotted him, and when the Pittsburgh Penguins drafted him in 1990, he became the first Czech player in history to play in the NHL.

Because of this, it was hard for Jaromír to fit in with his English-speaking teammates. He studied hard, though, and when he wasn't learning English through a tutor, he listened to a local Pittsburgh weather station so he could pick up words. When the Penguins signed Jiři Hrdina, also from the Czech Republic, Jaromír had someone to help him settle. They soon became known as the Czechmates!

We've had some spectacular impacts from rookies already in this book, but Jaromír's first two seasons in the NHL were something special. The Penguins reached their first Stanley Cup Finals in Jaromír's rookie season, winning it for the first time too! And then, to prove it wasn't a fluke, they won it again the following season, sweeping the Chicago Blackhawks in the Finals!

At 6-foot-3 and 230 pounds, Jaromír was a huge right-winger. One-on-one, there hasn't been many better. He had the option of dazzling his opponents with his mesmerizing skating, or if that didn't work, he could just go straight through them! He had that rare mix of grace and raw power. Even into his forties, he was a top forward, and he still holds the record as the oldest player in NHL history to score a hat trick, a feat he achieved at 45!

In his fifth season in the NHL, he won his first Art Ross Trophy after recording 70 points in the regular season. The following season was even more productive, and he ended the year with 140 points (62 goals and 87 assists)! By the 1997–98 season, Jaromír was the Penguins' captain, and in the following four years, he won four straight NHL scoring titles. If that wasn't enough, he also collected the Lester B. Pearson Award (1998) and the Hart Memorial Trophy (1999) and managed to squeeze in an Olympic gold medal in 1998 with the Czech Republic.

By 2001, Jaromír was the Penguins fans' star player. They loved him. But when the previously retired Mario Lemieux (we cover him next!) returned, things started to change. Mario was and is a Pittsburgh legend, and he was also captain before his retirement. Jaromír has never been the type of person just to roll over and let someone push him aside, but he also knew how loved and important Mario Lemieux was to the Penguins. It was felt that the town just wasn't big enough for the two of them, and that's how it proved to be. With the Penguins needing to cash in to save the franchise, Jaromír was traded to the Washington Capitals.

After signing what was then the biggest contract in the history of the NHL, Jaromír was expected to lead the Capitals to glory. It didn't work out that way, and his time in Washington was nothing short of a disaster. After three seasons, he was traded to the New York Rangers, who were thought to be a team on the slide.

Legendary Rangers captain Mark Messier retired as Jaromír's career in New York began, and many more of the franchise's top talents were moved on. It was a time of transition, and most of the media predicted the team would finish bottom. Jaromír disagreed, and he wasn't shy about telling people this either.

He started the season like a man possessed, scoring 10 goals in less than 10 games, an achievement only matched by three other players in NHL history. The Rangers defied all expectations (except that of Jaromír, of course!) and reached the Stanley Cup Playoffs. Unfortunately, Jaromír, who had been the team's driving force, picked up an injury in the first round, and the Rangers were eliminated by the New Jersey Devils.

Jaromír's high scoring continued as the seasons went by. In 2006, he registered his 1,400th point, and he played for the Rangers for another couple of years before becoming a free agent. When he signed for Russian team Avangard Omsk at the age of 37, it was felt that his time in the NHL was over. Of course, as we now know, Jaromír's talents seem to be timeless, and after three years in Russia, he returned to the States, signing for the Boston Bruins.

While there, he helped the team to the 2013 Stanley Cup Finals, where they lost 4–2 to the Blackhawks. It was a disappointing end to the season, but it did give Jaromír another record. He became the first player to play in two Stanley Cup Finals with a gap of 21 years between them!

Amazingly, more NHL trades followed, including seasons with the New Jersey Devils, the Florida Panthers, and the Calgary Flames. During his time at the Devils, Jaromír scored a hat trick at 45, an NHL record that will be very hard for anyone to beat.

After his time in the NHL, Jaromír returned to his hometown team, Rytiri Kladno, where he still plays today, even into his fifties. He is also the franchise's owner. The 2022–23 season was his 35th season as a pro. Now, how many hockey players can claim that particular achievement?

MARIO LEMIEUX

LE MAGNIFIQUE

TEAMS

PITTSBURGH
PENGUINS

1984–1997 & 2000–2006

CAREER STATS

NHL FIRST ALL-STAR TEAM	5
ART ROSS TROPHY	6
BILL MASTERTON MEMORIAL TROPHY	1
CALDER MEMORIAL TROPHY	1
CONN SMYTHE TROPHY	2
HART MEMORIAL TROPHY	3

STANLEY CUPS	GOALS	ASSISTS
2	690	1033

BIOGRAPHY

BORN	OCTOBER 5, 1965
NATIONALITY	CANADIAN
POSITION(S)	CENTRE
SHOT	RIGHT
RETIRED	2006

Known for his mesmerizing fakes and dekes, Mario Lemieux was a center of the highest quality. Nicknamed "The Magnificent One" and "Super Mario" (this one was obvious!), he spent his whole career with his beloved Pittsburgh Penguins. He won the Stanley Cup twice (alongside Jaromír Jágr) as a player and three more times as the franchise's owner!

Mario was born in Montreal on October 4, 1965. He showed promise early, and as a kid, he loved nothing more than practicing with his younger brother, Alain, who was also a very good player. Alain was signed by the Penguins for a season in 1986, but he only ever played one game.

As soon as he learned to walk, Mario was playing hockey. At the age of three, he could be found practicing with a wooden spoon and bottle caps. His family didn't have much money, so Mario's father built a mini rink in the front yard where Mario and his brothers could practice. Mario made the best of it, and pretty soon, there was a lot of talk around his hometown that he might be an NHL prospect.

Mario has never been shy when it comes to promoting himself. Even as a teenager, he told anyone who would listen that he would be a star. He always backed up his claims, as was proved when he broke several records during his junior career, including the most points ever in a season (282). Because of this, he might have expected to be drafted by one of the best teams in the NHL, but it didn't work out that way.

When the Penguins drafted Mario in 1984, they were a franchise in turmoil*. The team was broke and was averaging just 7,000 fans per game. This was only half of the Civic Arena's capacity. To make matters worse, they hadn't had a winning season since 1979.

But great players make great teams, and Mario's confidence and point-scoring were exactly what the Penguins needed. When he stole the puck off Hall of Famer Ray Bourque (yep, you guessed it—we'll cover him later!) on his debut and then scored with his first-ever shot in the NHL, the Penguins fans instantly had a new hero. Mario's rookie season was exceptional, as he finished with 100 points, played in the All-Star Game, was the first rookie to win the Game's MVP, and won the Calder Memorial Trophy.

His next season was even better, as he finished with 141 points, winning the Lester B. Pearson Award for his efforts. Unfortunately, the Penguins still hadn't caught up with Mario's talents (they soon would!), and the team failed to make the playoffs.

One of Mario's most impressive achievements was stopping Wayne Gretzky's dominance of the scoring title. He did so in the 1987–88 season when he racked up a staggering 168 points. The Penguins also had their first winning season in just under a decade but finished one point outside the playoffs. Things were starting to look up for the team.

If 168 points hadn't been enough, Mario smashed his own record the following season. He led the league in goals (85) and assists (114) to finish with an incredible 199 points. But ecstasy soon turned to agony, and a horrible back injury kept him out of a large chunk of the 1990–91 season. Luckily for Mario and the loyal Penguins fans, the team had Jaromír Jágr and future Hall of Famer Paul Coffey on their roster by then, and they were able to pick up the slack while Mario was recovering.

The Penguins finished first in the Eastern Conference, and when Mario returned from injury in time for the playoffs, everything fell into place. They went on to win the franchise's first Stanley Cup, with Mario being named Finals MVP in the process. All of his hard work had finally paid off, and the team that had struggled to half-fill their stadium when Mario arrived had won the biggest prize of all!

As we know from the Jaromír Jágr section, the Penguins retained their title the following season, sweeping the Blackhawks in the Finals.

Everyone who followed the NHL at the time knew that Mario Lemieux was tough, but even they were shocked by what he achieved in the 1992–93 season. After being diagnosed with Hodgkin's disease* midway through the season and then missing 20 games while he received radiation treatment*, Mario still somehow managed to top the scoring charts at the end of the year!

He had to miss the whole of the 1994–95 season as he continued to fight his illness, but he returned the following year to dominate the scoring charts once more, topping it in all categories on his way to claiming his third MVP award!

But his health continued to be a problem. Mario had been losing his passion for the game for a while too. He retired at the age of 31 to the sadness of the Penguins fans and was inducted into the Hall of Fame that same year. Without Mario's presence and popularity to keep the franchise afloat, the Penguins went into bankruptcy* a year after his retirement.

Seeing the franchise he loved in so much trouble hurt Mario. Along with some other investors, he bought the team and began a rebuild that would eventually see the Penguins have one of the most successful periods in their history. He also wanted to help on the ice, and he came out of retirement in time for the 2000–01 season, where he showed that none of his sharpness had left him when he registered an assist only 33 seconds into his return!

The Penguins were forced to sell most of their best players before the 2001–02 season as they tried to balance the books, which meant that Jaromír Jágr was traded. The team's form dipped, and they missed out on the playoffs for the next four seasons. Still, they were rebuilding, and the good times would soon return.

Mario retired from playing midway through the 2005–06 season following a string of injuries. He also wanted to run the franchise properly as owner, which he did so successfully, as the Penguins' three Stanley Cups under his leadership prove!

Outside of hockey, Mario does a lot for charity, especially his Mario Lemieux Foundation, which helps fund medical research. He also supports a whole list of other charities that would be too many to fit on these pages!

Mario Lemieux is a passionate man and one of the greatest players ever to play the game. He can also be considered the Penguins' savior, having taken them from the brink of collapse both as a player and then as an owner. He is a true sporting hero.

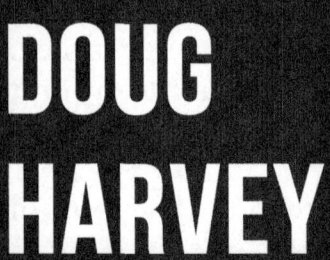

DOUG HARVEY

TEAMS

MONTREAL CANADIENS
1947–1961
↓
NEW YORK RANGERS
1961–1964
↓
DETROIT RED WINGS
1966–1967
↓
ST. LOUIS BLUES
1968–1969

STANLEY CUPS
6

CAREER STATS

NHL FIRST ALL-STAR TEAM	10
JAMES NORRIS MEMORIAL TROPHY	7
NHL ALL-STAR GAME	13
NHL SECOND ALL-STAR TEAM	1

GOALS	ASSISTS
88	452

BIOGRAPHY

BORN	DECEMBER 19, 1924
NATIONALITY	CANADIAN
POSITION(S)	DEFENCE
SHOT	LEFT
RETIRED	1969

Although he played for several teams throughout his career, Doug Harvey will always be best known for his time with the Montreal Canadiens. He spent the 1950s with that amazing team that dominated the decade and was one of their most loved players.

At a time when defensive players simply fired the puck as far forward as they could the moment they received it, Doug Harvey changed the game. He became one of the first defensemen to think about what he might do to help the team attack, and he often carried the puck forward before slipping a pass through to one of his teammates to score. His style of play was new and exciting.

Born in Montreal on December 19, 1924, Doug grew up near Notre-Dame-de-Grâce, a working-class neighborhood. His father worked in a warehouse, and young Doug was always an active kid. It is said that there wasn't a sport he wouldn't try, and when he did, he usually excelled.

Doug's childhood wasn't easy, though. His family struggled to pay the bills, and he often got in trouble for getting into fights at school. He spent his early mornings delivering newspapers as his family needed the extra money, so he was usually exhausted at the end of the day. Still, Doug always found time for hockey!

But any sport would do. In fact, he was so good at baseball that he was offered a contract by the Boston Braves in his late teens, but he turned them down. His first love was hockey, and he wanted to see if he could make it in the NHL!

It took Doug a while to get spotted, but only because he didn't really play organized hockey until his teens. Having started out as a goaltender, he was soon switched to defense. He was average height but stocky, and he loved the competitive side of defending.

Doug was soon spotted by the top NHL teams who wanted to sign him, but he had decided to go another way. World War II had been raging for a while, and as soon as Doug turned 18, he enrolled in the Navy. When his hockey talents were discovered, Doug was put onto the Navy's team in the hopes that his skills would boost morale. This didn't sit well with him, as he wanted to help fight for freedom. He asked to be sent to the front line, which he was in 1944.

When the war ended, Doug returned home and got himself back to full sharpness by playing minor league hockey for the Montreal Royals. He stayed there for a couple of years, leading them to the Allan Cup, before moving to the American Hockey League with the Buffalo Bisons. The move that would shape his career came soon after, and Doug became a Montreal Canadiens player in time for the 1947–48 season.

It took a few years for the Canadiens to reach their 1950s peak, and it would come at the same time that Gordie Howe was becoming a superstar with the Detroit Red Wings. In fact, Gordie and Doug would have some epic battles throughout the decade, with both players at the height of their powers!

The Canadiens reached the Stanley Cup Finals in 1951 and '52 but lost them both, the second a humiliating 4–0 defeat to Gordie and the Red Wings. Amazingly, the Canadiens would go on to appear in every single Stanley Cup Finals in the 1950s. Ten consecutive finals appearances! Now that's dominance.

Their first victorious final that decade came in the 1953 Finals when they beat the Boston Bruins 4–1. They lost an epic battle over seven games to the Red Wings the following year and then repeated that result the next season. They got their revenge on the Red Wings in 1956 and then retained their title in '57, smashing the Bruins again. They then beat the Bruins again and the Maple Leafs twice more to make it five Stanley Cups in a row!

All through this period of dominance, Doug was named to the All-Star team every single year. He also won the James Norris Memorial Trophy six times and was considered the best defenseman in the business. Despite all of this, Doug was somehow blamed for the Canadiens' loss in the 1961 playoffs, a game that is generally seen as the end of that dynasty.

He took the comments to heart, and after falling out with the general manager, he was quickly traded to the New York Rangers. In his late thirties, Doug was convinced to sign for the Rangers as the team's player-coach. It was a role that never suited him, as he was always a player who liked to be one of the guys. He was his teammates' pal, not the man who told them what to do.

Still, in his first year as player-coach, he won the Norris Trophy (his last), making him the first Rangers player to ever win it. He also led the team to the playoffs for the first time in five years, but he left the role before the 1962–63 season. After that, his career faded pretty rapidly.

Doug Harvey's life off the ice was never as smooth as it was on it. At a time when mental health issues weren't discussed, especially in men, Doug had to suffer in silence. In truth, he probably never knew what was really wrong with him, as things like depression weren't as widely understood as they are today.

He was inducted into the Hall of Fame in 1973, and the Montreal Canadiens retired his number 2 jersey in 1985. Doug passed away four years after that at just 65, but his legacy will always live on. He remains tied with Nicklas Lidstrom with seven Norris Trophies and only one behind Bobby Orr. That's pretty good company to keep!

MAURICE RICHARD

THE COMET

TEAMS

MONTREAL CANADIENS

1942–1960

CAREER STATS

FIRST TEAM ALL-STAR	8
HART MEMORIAL TROPHY	1
SECOND TEAM ALL-STAR	6
CANADIAN PRESS MALE ATHLETE OF THE YEAR	3
LOU MARSH TROPHY	1

STANLEY CUPS	GOALS	ASSISTS
8	544	422

BIOGRAPHY

BORN	AUGUST 4, 1921
NATIONALITY	CANADIAN
POSITION(S)	RIGHT WING
SHOT	LEFT
RETIRED	1960

If Doug Harvey was the raw power of that Canadiens dynasty, then Maurice Richard was the grace. And if Doug Harvey's six Stanley Cup victories are impressive, then Maurice's eight are mind-blowing! The two of them were exceptional at different ends of the rink, but they are both NHL legends.

Maurice Richard was born on August 4, 1921, in Montreal, a city that seems to produce an endless stream of world-class hockey players. As one of eight children, Maurice didn't have much growing up. He was born in the 1920s, a time when America, Canada, and the whole world were falling into the Great Depression. As we briefly discussed in the Gordie Howe section, this was an awful period in history.

Things were so bad that Maurice grew up malnourished* due to his poor diet and terrible living conditions. When he was given a pair of skates at the age of four, they became an escape for him. Being out on the ice, feeling the wind on his face, Maurice could pretend that everything was okay in the world. And when the local lakes thawed each year, his father would create a mini rink in the backyard for the kids.

Maurice didn't get to play organized hockey until his teens, as the family couldn't afford it. And when he finally did get there, because of his ill health, often the other kids were a lot bigger and stronger. In fact,

Maurice's health problems affected him all through his adulthood and NHL career, but he refused to let it hold him back.

Like so many sportspeople who come up through hard times, Maurice used his problems to spur him on. He pushed himself harder than the kid next to him, and when one of them was stronger, he made sure he became tougher than them. When things got rough, he got rougher.

When Maurice was 14, his younger brother Henri was born. This is important because Henri would grow up to be a phenomenal player who would also spend his entire career with the Canadiens. Not only that, but he would become his big brother's teammate for the last five years of Maurice's career!

Maurice had dropped out of school at 16 to work as a machinist* with his father to help pay the bills, so he had to split his time between the factory and practice. His hard work and determination paid off when he was picked up by the Montreal Canadiens in his late teens. They moved him to their affiliate when he turned 18, but his injury problems struck on his very first game when he broke his ankle, meaning he would miss the whole season.

Devastated but not beaten, Maurice worked hard on his recovery. He got back to full fitness for the 1941–42 season, but the Canadiens felt he wasn't ready and sent him to their affiliate once more. He recorded an admirable 17 points in 31 games before injury struck again, this time a broken wrist. Despite this heartbreak, Maurice was making a name for himself as a good left-winger. The only fear was that he'd never be injury-free.

With World War II taking a lot of players overseas to help fight for their country, combined with low attendance at Canadiens games due to the team's poor performances, Maurice was given a shot. He killed it at the tryouts and was handed the number 15 jersey. He scored his first goal soon after, but another injury struck him down midway through his rookie season.

To make matters worse, the ankle he broke a couple of years before never set right. It remained misshapen, which forced Maurice to change his skating style from the one he'd known since he was a kid. He doubled up on his training, both to get used to his new style and to get as fit as possible for the new season. Around this time, his daughter Huguette was born, and Maurice changed his jersey number to 9 to match her weight—nine pounds.

His training paid off, and he had his first injury-free year. Not only that, but he played superbly, quickly becoming a fan favorite due to his talents and passion. When coach Dick Irvin moved him from left wing to right wing before the 1943–44 season, everything seemed to fall into place. Alongside Toe Blake and Elmer Lach, the trio formed the formidable frontline known as the Punch Line.

The Canadiens won the 1944 Stanley Cup, sweeping the Blackhawks in the Finals. It was the franchise's first Stanley Cup victory in 13 years and the first of Maurice's eight! Maurice dominated in the playoffs, racking up 12 points, including 5 in one game against the Maple Leafs.

By the following season, Maurice was seen as one of the best players in the world. His scoring had really taken off, and he was constantly setting new records. When he scored five goals and three assists in a 9–1 demolition of the Red Wings, he became the first player to register eight points in a single game. He ended that season as the first player in the NHL to finish with 50-plus points, and we have to remember this was before the Expansion Era*, so there were fewer games.

After a disappointing loss in the playoffs, the Canadiens returned to the Stanley Cup Finals in 1946 and beat the Bruins to lift the trophy for the second time in two years. A Canadiens dynasty was expected, but it didn't come for a while. In fact, they had to wait until 1953 to win it again (Doug Harvey's first!), and the dynasty began.

As we saw in the previous section, the Canadiens reached the Finals every year for a decade, winning the last five in a row. Maurice was captain for the final four of these, playing alongside his baby brother!

Due to his silky skills on the ice, Maurice was often stopped by increasingly rougher tactics. He sometimes reacted, which meant he got in many fights during games. One such incident led to the Canadiens fans rioting, an event that is still remembered today as the Richard Riot!

Maurice Richard continued to suffer injuries throughout his career, but they were never as bad as the early days. He managed to play at the top level until he was 39 before becoming the Canadiens' vice president in 1964. This role never really suited him, and he left it after only a year. He always stayed close to the team he loved, and when he passed away in 2000, the Canadiens lost one of their truest legends.

GUY LAFLEUR

THE FLOWER

TEAMS

MONTREAL CANADIENS
1971–1985

NEW YORK RANGERS
1988–1989

QUEBEC NORDIQUES
1989–1991

STANLEY CUPS
5

CAREER STATS

FIRST-TEAM ALL-STAR	6
ART ROSS TROPHY	3
CONN SMYTHE TROPHY	1
HART MEMORIAL TROPHY	2
TED LINDSAY AWARD	3
MOLSON CUP	7

GOALS	ASSISTS
560	793

BIOGRAPHY

BORN	SEPTEMBER 20, 1951
NATIONALITY	CANADIAN
POSITION(S)	RIGHT WING
SHOT	RIGHT
RETIRED	1991

The dominance of the Montreal Canadiens in the NHL can be broken into sections, like the Doug Harvey and Maurice Richard team of the fifties. The Canadiens have always had their moments in the Stanley Cup (well, up until the early nineties!), and that dominance between 1950 and 1960 wasn't the only time they were the best. They had another fantastic period in the seventies, and Guy Lafleur was a massive part of that success.

The man nicknamed "The Flower" or "Le Demon Blond" was the first player to score 50-plus goals in six consecutive seasons, and even though he played briefly for the New York Rangers and the Quebec Nordiques near the end of his career, he is best known for his time with the Canadiens.

Born in Thurso, Quebec, on September 20, 1941, Guy fell in love with hockey from the moment he woke up on his fifth Christmas and found a stick under the tree. From then on, it was rarely out of his hands. He practiced all the time and broke many records for his school team.

He played for three seasons in the Quebec International Pee-Wee Hockey Tournaments, scoring a tournament record 64 points in his final year. His impressive performances saw him snapped up by the Quebec Remparts of the Quebec Major Junior Hockey

League, and he led them to the Memorial Cup in 1971, scoring a staggering 130 goals along the way!

His idol growing up was Bobby Orr, the Bruins and Blackhawks legend who will appear in this book very soon. Bobby Orr has always been a hockey idol, and Guy loved him. What is strange about this is that Bobby was a world-class defenseman, while Guy preferred to attack. He played right wing, and he was phenomenal.

After his unbelievable scoring in the 1971 Memorial Cup, Guy was one of the hottest prospects in that year's NHL draft. He was selected by the Canadiens as a first-draft choice, picking the number 10 jersey.

Now, we discussed the pressures of being a prospect in sport in the Sidney Crosby section, and Guy was one of the young men who really felt the pressure early on. In fact, in his first three years with the Canadiens, he didn't get much time on the ice. He struggled with the expectations, and it was pretty hard back then to break into the Canadiens' team. It's always stacked with superstars, including Hall of Famer Henri Richard, brother of our last entrant, Maurice Richard!

Guy was part of the Canadiens' team that won the 1973 Stanley Cup, but his real breakthrough came the following year. He had worked hard to develop his now famous skating style—smooth and with a great scoring touch. When his calm nature was added into the mix, he was a real force to be reckoned with. Defenders would try to hack at him, hook him, and slash, but he never retaliated, which made them furious!

Guy Lafleur was a major part of the Canadiens team that won four Stanley Cups in a row between 1976 and 1979, winning playoff MVP in '77. But his talents didn't stretch as far as he thought, and he released an awful disco album (ask your grandparents about disco music!) in 1979 called Lafleur! The album was just Guy giving out hockey instructions over a lame beat! If you can find it online, have a listen—but be prepared to cringe!

As the seventies became the eighties, Guy's talents began to fade with age. As they did, the Canadiens started to wane*. The team would have moments of greatness again when Patrick Roy broke through, but never the dominance of the fifties, sixties, and seventies. In Guy's 1980–81 season, he failed to score 50 or more goals for the first time since 1973–74.

The next three seasons saw the Canadiens suffer first-round exits every year, and then the fourth brought the franchise's first losing record of the Expansion Era.

When defensive-minded coach Jacques Lemaire was hired in the mid-eighties, he and Guy instantly clashed. When things got so bad that Guy had to ask for a trade, general manager Serge Savard refused his request. Serge knew the fans would be furious if he let a future Hall of Famer leave, but Guy was insistent. When he wasn't allowed to leave, he retired.

His Hall of Fame induction came a few years later, and Guy followed it up with the shock announcement that he was coming out of retirement. He signed for the New York Rangers and then the Quebec Nordiques. His time with both franchises was pretty uneventful, but it did take him back to his beloved Canadiens whenever the teams played each other.

Despite the bad taste that had been left in the fans' mouths when Guy left, his return to the Montreal Forum was like a dream. The home crowd cheered every time he touched the puck, and he even managed to score twice. The old chant of "GUY! GUY! GUY!" was sung throughout the game, and the joy could be seen on Guy's face. He was home!

Following his retirement in 1991, Guy had many business ventures. He started his own energy drink company (Flower Power) and built a successful chain of restaurants.

Sadly, a devastating week for hockey in 2022 saw the NHL lose two of its all-time greats when Guy Lafleur passed away a few days after Mike Bossy. Guy was a hero to the Canadiens fans, which is not an easy thing to achieve, given how many legends have played for the team.

Guy's grace and easy scoring style made him stand out, and the millions of players since who have tried to copy it have never quite been able to do so. Guy Lafleur was one of a kind!

BOBBY HULL

THE GOLDEN JET

TEAMS

CHICAGO
BLACK HAWKS
1957–1972

WINNIPEG JETS
1972–1979

HARTFORD
WHALERS
1979–1980

STANLEY CUPS
1

CAREER STATS

NHL FIRST ALL–STAR TEAM	10
ART ROSS TROPHY	3
HART MEMORIAL TROPHY	2
LADY BYNG MEMORIAL TROPHY	1
LESTER PATRICK TROPHY	1
AVCO CUP	3

GOALS	ASSISTS
610	560

BIOGRAPHY	BORN	JANUARY 3, 1939
	NATIONALITY	CANADIAN
	POSITION(S)	LEFT WING
	SHOT	LEFT
	RETIRED	1980

Now we have a left-winger who was so good he became the first player to have opposing players shadow him. Before Bobby Hull, the idea of a defenseman spending the whole game glued to an attacking player was unheard of. Bobby Hull starred for the Blackhawks his whole career alongside his baby brother Dennis, who wasn't so bad himself!

Nicknamed the "Golden Jet" due to his blond hair and fast-paced skating skills, Bobby Hull was also famed for his powerful slap shot. A left-winger who scored as well as provided, he managed to lead the NHL scoring chart seven times!

Bobby was born in Point Anne, Ontario, on January 3, 1939, and he had to come through some tough times. World War II was beginning, and the family had to survive on his father's factory-worker salary. One of his only escapes was hockey, and he played every chance he could get.

His junior career started in Belleville, a nearby city, where he was spotted by scouts from the Woodstock Warriors. Bobby signed up for their Junior B team in 1954. After some fantastic performances, he was promoted to the Warriors A Team before the year was out, and he helped them win the Sutherland Cup as Ontario champions.

After being picked up by the Chicago Blackhawks as a teenager, Bobby was sent out to a couple of their affiliates, the Galt Black Hawks and the St. Catharines Teepees in the Ontario Hockey Association. His time there was spent perfecting his raw skills, and when he turned 18, the Chicago Blackhawks thought he was ready for the main stage!

Bobby's rookie season was terrific. He finished second in the voting for the Calder Memorial Trophy and became an instant favorite among the fans. At first, Bobby wore the number 7 jersey and then the number 16. When the number 9 jersey became available, he snapped it up. His hero Gordie Howe wore 9, and Bobby wanted to be just like him.

By the 1959–60 season (Bobby's third in the NHL), he led the league in both goals and assists and won the Art Ross Trophy for his efforts. He managed to win it again in 1962 and '66! Bobby also helped the Blackhawks win their first Stanley Cup in 23 years in 1961, beating the Red Wings and his hero Gordie Howe 4–2 in the Finals!

One year before the Expansion Era, when there were fewer teams to play against, Bobby Hull became the first player to register a 50-goal season. In fact, his 51st goal that season, in a game against the New York Rangers, brought a seven-minute standing ovation from the home fans. He finished the season with 54 goals, and with the Expansion Era starting the following year, his record will stand forever.

Oh, and Bobby also set the record for most points that year, finishing with 97. Both of his records in the

Original Six* era will always be intact.

In his 15 full NHL seasons, Bobby was voted First Team All-Star left-winger 10 times, and during this period, his slap shot was recorded at 118 miles per hour! He could skate at just under 30 miles per hour, and what might be even more impressive is that his wrist shot was said to be even harder than his slap shot!

With rumors of the World Hockey Association (WHA) starting up in 1972, Bobby decided to test the waters. He had been annoyed at his low salary for a while, and he had heard that the WHA franchises might be willing to pay big bucks for the top talent from the NHL. In a statement most people believed to be a joke, he said he would join the WHA if one of the franchises were willing to pay him a million dollars!

Amazingly, the Winnipeg Jets agreed to his terms, and Bobby signed on as player-manager in a 10-year deal worth $1.75 million, with a cool million upfront. It was unheard of, and even though it doesn't seem like much compared to modern-day players, it was huge back then. When Bobby was joined in the WHA by his hero, Gordie Howe, he surely felt like he had made the right decision.

His time with the Jets was massively successful, and he won the Gordie Howe Trophy (remember that!) twice, in 1973 and '75. He formed a devastating front line with Swedish stars Anders Hedberg and Ulf Nilsson that became known as "The Hot Line." In both of Bobby's MVP seasons, the Jets won the AVCO Cup (Stanley Cup equivalent in the WHA) each year. Also, the 1975 season was Bobby's most productive as a pro. He registered 77 goals and 65 assists for a total of 142 points.

Bobby was the only WHA player on the Canada team for the inaugural* Canada Cup in 1976. Canada won it, which wasn't surprising when the team had stars such as Bobby Orr, Phil Esposito, and Bobby himself on it. It was yet another fantastic achievement, but his skills on the ice were starting to be affected by his age.

He played here and there for the Jets through the late seventies and retired soon after. When the WHA folded and the leagues were merged*, Bobby came out of retirement so he could play in the NHL again. He managed 18 games for the Jets before he was traded to the Hartford Whalers, where he was teamed up with Gordie Howe, who was 51 at the time! Bobby played nine games with his hero before retiring for the second and last time.

Bobby Hull ended his career with 610 goals and 560 assists (1,170 points), three Art Ross Trophies, two Hart Memorial Trophies, two Gordie Howe Trophies, the 1976 Canada Cup, and the 1961 Stanley Cup! In 1978, he was made an Officer of the Order of Canada, and the Blackhawks retired his number 9 jersey not long after his retirement.

He might have only won the Stanley Cup once, but Bobby did so much more for hockey than win. He changed how attacking players are defended, which is an astonishing achievement!

BOBBY ORR

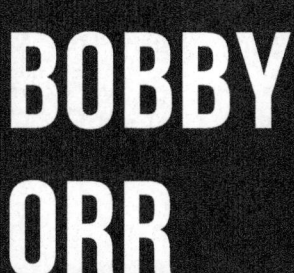

NUMBER FOUR

TEAMS

BOSTON BRUINS
1966-1976

CHICAGO BLACK HAWKS
1976-1979

STANLEY CUPS
2

CAREER STATS

ART ROSS TROPHY	2
CALDER MEMORIAL TROPHY	1
CONN SMYTHE TROPHY	2
HART MEMORIAL TROPHY	3
JAMES NORRIS MEMORIAL TROPHY	8
LESTER PATRICK TROPHY	1

GOALS	ASSISTS
270	645

BIOGRAPHY

BORN	**MARCH 20, 1948**
NATIONALITY	**CANADIAN**
POSITION(S)	**DEFENCE**
SHOT	**LEFT**
RETIRED	**1979**

Bobby Orr has been mentioned so often in this book that it might feel like we've covered him already, but he's popped up so many times because he is a true legend. Before Bobby, being a defenseman wasn't cool. It was seen as boring and a position that only involved brute strength. Bobby changed that, becoming the only defenseman in the history of the NHL to win the Art Ross Trophy. And he did it twice!

Bobby was born on March 20, 1948, in Parry Sound, a small town on the shores of Georgian Bay, Ontario. His ancestors were Irish, his grandfather having emigrated to Canada years before. Sport was in his family, and his grandfather was a professional soccer player before moving to Canada.

Bobby's father was also athletic and was considered a top prospect in his youth. He was offered a chance to join the Atlantic City Sea Gulls but turned it down to join the Royal Canadian Navy and fight in World War II. Bobby was born a few years after the war ended but wasn't expected to live very long.

A sickly baby, Bobby always seemed to have to fight from the day he was born. When he first put on skates and picked up a stick, his parents worried. Even at five, he was small and frail for his age, and they feared for his health. When he began playing organized hockey a few years later, they knew it was in his blood. Bobby knew he was at a disadvantage due to his size, so he concentrated on improving the parts of his game that his body would allow, namely his agility and speed.

His size also meant that he played on the front line as a kid, but some of his coaches saw how competitive he was, and he was soon switched to defense. Having already polished his attacking skills, Bobby started to add them to his defensive game, often skating forward with the puck before slotting it into the net. That style of play had never been seen before, and it brought him to the attention of many scouts.

One of the first NHL franchises to try to sign him was the Boston Bruins, and they did so from as early as 1962 when Bobby was just 14. Soon after, the Red Wings, the Canadiens, and the Maple Leafs all showed an interest. The Bruins were in a bad state at the time, having not won the Stanley Cup in more than two decades and not even making the playoffs in years. Bobby could have chosen one of the more successful teams, but he picked the Bruins, as they tried the hardest to sign him.

As soon as he signed at 14, Bobby was thrown into junior games against 18 and 19-year-olds. He still managed to set records, including the most goals by a defenseman in a season (29). The following seasons at junior level saw improvements every year, and by his fourth, he recorded 38 goals and 56 assists for a total of 94 points!

Bobby was given his shot with the Bruins for the 1966–67 season, with the team still yet to reach the playoffs. They were really struggling, and attendance had dropped dramatically. By the end of Bobby's rookie season, the crowds had grown by an average of 41,000 people! The Bruins finished last again, but Bobby's attacking flair from defense was new and exciting, and the Bruins fans had a new idol.

That rookie season saw him score 13 goals and 28 assists while also picking up the Calder Memorial Trophy, but his second season was a reality check.

Bobby picked up several injuries and only managed 46 games, but he still registered 11 goals and 20 assists. The Bruins had added more talent to their roster, including Phil Esposito (remember him!), Ken Hodge, and Fred Stanfield, so things were looking up. Despite Bobby's injuries, the team reached the playoffs for the first time in years.

By the 1969–70 season, Bobby was one of the most electrifying players in the world. He doubled his best scoring record, topping 120 points, and finished top scorer. He ended the season with the first of his two Art Ross Trophies, becoming the first and only defenseman to do so. In the playoffs, he racked up nine goals and 11 assists, including one of the most famous goals in NHL history against the St. Louis Blues in the Finals.

In what has been described as the greatest moment in Boston's sporting history, Bobby Orr "took flight!" After exchanging passes with Derek Sanderson, Bobby flicked the puck into the net just as he was tripped. He flew forward, Superman style, with his arms splayed out in front of him. One of the photographers at the game took a picture as Bobby was in midair, and it is an image that will stand the test of time.

It was also fitting that Bobby should be the game (and series) winner, and the Bruins lifted their first Stanley Cup in 41 years as they swept the Blues.

The following season, he recorded 139 points (37 goals and 102 assists), and the one after that, 117, finishing second behind his teammate Phil Esposito in the scoring chart. He finished that season with the Hart Memorial and Norris Trophies on his way to another Stanley Cup victory, which would be his second and last.

The early seventies saw change at the Bruins as a number of the NHL's top players left for the WHA. The Bruins suffered more than most, but Bobby still maintained his own high standards, finishing the 1972–73 season with 101 points as the Bruins lost in the playoffs. They finished first in the division the following season but lost to the Philadelphia Flyers over six games in that year's Stanley Cup.

The 1974–75 season was an amazing one for Bobby personally. He won the Art Ross Trophy for the second and last time in his career. He also broke his own record for goals, scoring an astonishing 46. He added 89 assists to that total, meaning he had reached the 100-plus point mark for six consecutive seasons.

Bobby's last year with the Bruins (1975–76) wasn't nice. He underwent surgery before the season began, and he was never the same again. When his contract ran down, the Bruins didn't renew it, and he signed for the Chicago Blackhawks. More injuries restricted him to just 26 games over three years in Chicago, and he missed the entire 1977–78 season.

Bobby Orr retired with 270 goals and 645 assists (915 points) in just 657 games, which was simply unheard of for a defenseman until Ray Bourque came along. The Bruins retired Bobby's number 4 jersey, and the man who was known for being extremely shy and kind-hearted off the ice was inducted into the NHL Hall of Fame a year after he retired at just 31!

Bobby has always been known as a kind man, and many of his ex-teammates have spoken of how he helped them through tough times. There are a few players on this list that might never be equaled, but with Bobby Orr, it's not really a question. Was there ever a defenseman as attacking as Bobby Orr? Probably not, although Ray Bourque fans might disagree!

ALEXANDER OVECHKIN

OVI

TEAMS

DYNAMO MOSCOW
2001–2005

⬇

WASHINGTON CAPITALS
2005–2023*

STANLEY CUPS
1

CAREER STATS

NHL FIRST ALL-STAR TEAM	8
ART ROSS TROPHY	1
CALDER MEMORIAL TROPHY	1
CONN SMYTHE TROPHY	1
HART MEMORIAL TROPHY	3
MAURICE "ROCKET" RICHARD TROPHY	9

GOALS	ASSISTS
827*	674*

BIOGRAPHY

BORN	17 SEPTEMBER 1985
NATIONALITY	RUSSIAN
POSITION(S)	LEFT WING
SHOT	RIGHT
RETIRED	STILL PLAYING

Another one of our entrants who was still playing when this book was written, Alex Ovechkin is a goal machine. The third player in history to score 800 goals in regular season play, he recently surpassed the great Gordie Howe for total goals. The man nicknamed "Ovi" came to America with one dream: to play in the NHL. He not only achieved his dream but surpassed it.

Alexander Ovechkin was born in Moscow on September 17, 1985, and his family believed from that day he was destined for greatness. His parents were top athletes; his mother won gold in basketball at the Olympic Games in 1976 and '80, while his father was a professional soccer player.

Alex's mother has since said that from the moment her boy picked up a hockey stick at the age of two, they knew that was his destiny. They weren't wrong. Alex lived and breathed hockey, constantly playing outside or watching the NHL on TV whenever it was shown on Russian sports channels.

Growing up, Alex's family struggled to make ends meet. They lived in Russia at a time when things were very tough, especially for working-class families, and their crumbling high-rise building overlooked barren land. Alex attended public school number 596, a place that was known for being seriously strict. He often suffered violence at the hands of the principal.

His parents worked long hours, so Alex's older brother Sergei often had to bring Alex to his games when he was a kid. Alex loved his brother, and he credits Sergei with giving him his love of hockey. When Sergei died in a car crash at the age of 17, poor Alex was only eight. Despite how heartbroken Alex was, his parents insisted that he play in his team's game the following day.

Alex never got over the loss of his brother. He continues to kiss his glove and point to the sky when he scores a goal in honor of Sergei.

His youth career continued to grow, and rapidly at that. Alex based his game on his idol, Mario Lemieux, and Super Mario's influence can still be seen in Alex's game today. Alex was signed by local team HC Dynamo Moscow, and he took off like a rocket, shooting up through the developmental system. When he broke the junior team's record by scoring 56 goals in a season, he was moved up to the senior team. He was only 16!

Even though he was still a teenager, he got plenty of ice time. He made his Russian Superleague debut at 16, and in his three years at Dynamo, he scored an impressive 36 goals and 32 assists in 152 games.

The hype around Alex was massive, and when the 2004 NHL Entry Draft came around, most franchises wanted him. The Washington Capitals won out, and he was selected first overall. Unfortunately, Alex signed just before an NHL lockout, so he had to put his dream of playing in the NHL on hold. He returned to HC Dynamo Moscow for another season to keep himself sharp.

Alex's NHL moment finally came on October 5, 2005, when he stepped out onto the ice in a game against the Columbus Blue Jackets. He wasted no time and scored two points in a 3–2 win. A couple of months later, he bagged his first hat trick, this time against the Mighty Ducks in another victory.

Three days later, Alex scored what is considered by many to be one of the greatest NHL goals in history when he was tripped by defenseman Paul Mara, only to somehow hook the puck as he slid, using only one hand, before slotting it into the net. It has since become known as "The Goal," which says it all.

Alex ended his rookie season with the Calder Memorial Trophy, and he was a finalist in the Lester B. Pearson Award voting.

His second season was even more impressive, and his skills as a left-winger were being talked about a lot. Alex is a goal scorer and a creator, proven when he finished the year with 46 goals and 46 assists. He also ended the season with his first All-Star appearance, but he needed more.

Like so many on this list, Alex stayed with franchises that weren't even close to his level because he was loyal. The Capitals finished dead last in both of his first two seasons, and Alex could have easily asked for a trade. Every team in the NHL would have wanted him, but he loved the Capitals, and he wanted to win trophies in Washington and nowhere else.

His loyalty paid off, and after some good business in the off-season, the Capitals shocked everyone by winning the division title! It helped that Alex scored an incredible 65 goals, and even though the team lost in the first-round playoff, Alex knew they were on the up. He ended the season with the Hart Memorial Trophy.

The Capitals continued to improve, winning the division title again the following season (2008–09). This time, they reached the Conference semifinals but fell short against that Sidney Crosby-inspired Penguins team. Alex's high scoring continued to drag the Capitals into the playoffs, but the team always fell just short of the Stanley Cup Finals, losing in the Conference semifinals twice more.

Alex won his third Hart Memorial Trophy at the end of the 2012–13 season, but Stanley Cup glory continued to evade him. It would be such a tragedy for a player of Alex's talents to never win the trophy he chased since he was two, and for a while, it looked like his loyalty to the Capitals might do just that. But fate had other plans, and Alex finally got his hands on the Stanley Cup in 2018!

In what was the Washington Capitals' first Stanley Cup victory in over two decades, Alex Ovechkin performed miracles on the ice over five games. His 15th playoff goal sealed the winning game at the expense of the Vegas Golden Knights, and Alex became the first Russian player in NHL history to captain a team to Stanley Cup glory. He was awarded the Conn Smythe Trophy at the end.

The following year, Alex helped the Capitals win their fourth-straight division title but lost in the playoffs and couldn't retain their Stanley Cup.

In the 2022–23 season, Alex scored his 802nd goal to surpass Gordie Howe, leaving only Wayne Gretzky ahead of him. Alex might be a bit behind The Great One, but maybe he can catch him! We'll have to wait and see!

TERRY SAWCHUK

UKEY

TEAMS

DETROIT RED WINGS
1949–1955
↓
BOSTON BRUINS
1955–1957
↓
DETROIT RED WINGS
1957–1964
↓
TORONTO MAPLE LEAFS
1964–1967
↓
LOS ANGELES KINGS
1967–1968
↓
DETROIT RED WINGS
1968–1969
↓
NEW YORK RANGERS
1969–1970

STANLEY CUPS
4

CAREER STATS

NHL FIRST ALL-STAR TEAM	3
CALDER MEMORIAL TROPHY	1
LESTER PATRICK TROPHY	1
VEZINA TROPHY	4
NHL ALL-STAR GAME	11
NHL SECOND ALL-STAR TEAM	4

SO	GAA
103	2.50

BIOGRAPHY

BORN	DECEMBER 28, 1929
NATIONALITY	CANADIAN
POSITION(S)	GOALTENDER
CAUGHT	LEFT
RETIRED	1970

As our second and final goaltender on the list, Terry Sawchuk's story is as sad as it is inspiring. He came along at a time when NHL goalies didn't wear protective masks, and some of his injuries were horrendous. It was also a time when mental health wasn't really understood, and Terry really suffered because of it. But he never gave less than 100% and continued to put his body on the line up until the day he died.

Terrence Sawchuk was born on December 28, 1929, in the North End of Winnipeg before his family moved to Bowman Avenue when Terry was a child. Bowman was a tough, working-class neighborhood, and the family struggled to pay the bills. Terry's father was a tinsmith, and the Sawchuks often went hungry.

Terry's brother died of scarlet fever when he was a kid, and then his older brother and hero, Paul, passed away when he was 17. Paul had been a top goaltender, too, and his death hit Terry hard.

When Terry was 12, he broke his elbow playing rugby. Because his parents had told him not to play that day, he hid his injury, not knowing it was broken. Without medical treatment, Terry's bones didn't heal properly, and they set crooked. It was an injury that would affect him his whole career.

Terry was great at several sports, including football, baseball, and rugby. When his friend gave him some old goaltending equipment, Terry quickly forgot about them all and fell in love with hockey. His junior career took off quickly, and Terry was being scouted by several of the NHL's top franchises before his teens.

In fact, a scout from the Detroit Red Wings offered him a tryout when he was only 14, and he did so well that the team offered Terry an amateur contract. Four years later, Terry had signed a pro deal.

Now that he was an official Red Wings player, Terry quickly rose through the ranks in the developmental system. He even played a few games for the Red Wings in 1947, when he was only 18 after starting goalie Harry Lumley got injured. Terry impressed so much that the Red Wings felt comfortable trading Lumley to the Blackhawks at the end of the season.

Now, we have to remember that this was a time when teams didn't have backup goalies. The Red Wings were putting their fate in Terry, even though he was still a rookie. It should also be noted that the Red Wings had just won the Stanley Cup with Lumley as goaltender, so the pressure on Terry was huge.

Terry became the Red Wings' starting goalie for the 1950–51 season, and in his first five years, the team won the Stanley Cup three times. With Terry keeping the goals out and Gordie Howe slapping them in at the other end, the Red Wings were a force. But things weren't always good for Terry. He suffered from severe depression his whole life, and as we've discussed earlier in the book, the information on such things as depression and anxiety back then wasn't anything like it is today. Terry had to suffer in silence, and he was often in a very dark place, even as his team won Stanley Cups.

As his career progressed, so did the number of injuries he picked up. With no backup goaltenders, Terry had to play through the pain and somehow managed to be selected for the All-Star Game in each of his first five years as a pro.

With his depression worsening, Terry found some comfort in food. After gaining a little weight, Red Wings' head coach Jack Adams told reporters that Terry needed to lose weight. The humiliation only made Terry's depression worse, and he not only lost the weight he'd gained but many more pounds on top. He was skinny and sickly, which made his injuries even worse.

Some of the injuries he picked up over the years included a broken foot, severe cuts and bruises, ruptured discs in his back, elbow issues (requiring three operations), a collapsed lung, and severed tendons in his hand. Altogether, he had more than 400 stitches on his face, including his eyeball, yet his sacrifices seemed to mean nothing to the Red Wings.

Shockingly, after only five full seasons in Detroit, they traded him to the Boston Bruins. The trade broke Terry's heart, which was made worse by the horrible time he had at the Bruins. His injuries had piled up, and his depression had gotten even worse. He was frail and miserable, and when he retired in his late twenties after three seasons in Boston, team executives and reporters called him a quitter. It was a disgusting way to talk about someone who was suffering so much.

Realizing their mistake, the Red Wings re-signed him in 1957, and he came out of retirement. He spent seven years there, but the Red Wings weren't the same force they had been and wouldn't be for a long, long time. Following his second spell in Detroit, Terry was released in 1964 when his contract ran down. He was signed by the Maple Leafs, where he formed a bizarre yet highly effective partnership with fellow veteran goalie Johnny Bower.

Bower was 40 then, and it was decided that he would share game time with Terry. It worked a treat, and in their first season together, Terry and Johnny claimed the Vezina Trophy, the award given at the end of the season for the fewest goals allowed! And it got even better for Terry when his unbelievable performances in the Stanley Cup Finals helped the Maple Leafs win the title. In Game 6, Terry stopped 40 of 41 shots in a 3–1 win over the Canadiens.

It was Terry's fourth and final Stanley Cup, but maybe the sweetest, seeing as he had been written off so many times in the past.

Following his time with the Maple Leafs, Terry had short spells with the Los Angeles Kings, the Red Wings again (a single season and his third spell in Detroit), and finally, the New York Rangers.

While at the Rangers, Terry got in a drunken fight with teammate Ron Stewart. He sustained an injury that gradually worsened, and after having his gallbladder removed, his body started to fail. Before he died, Terry told reporters the fight had been nothing more than horseplay and that Ron Stewart was completely innocent. Ron was quickly proven innocent but losing such a fantastic goaltender sent shockwaves through the NHL.

Terry Sawchuk was one of the bravest players in the history of any sport. He managed a then-record 447 wins and 103 shutouts in his career, and he will always be remembered as one of the greatest goaltenders to ever play the game. The only battle Terry could never win was with his depression. If he'd played hockey today, he surely would have gotten the help he needed. Unfortunately, the world lost a legend far too early, but we can honor him by remembering his unique skills.

Always remember that mental health is so important. If you ever feel sad, make sure you talk to someone. It could be a parent, an aunt, a grandparent, or a teacher. Just don't suffer in silence. Terry Sawchuk would want you to find your happiness like he never could!

JEAN BÉLIVEAU

LE GROS BILL

TEAMS

MONTREAL CANADIENS
1950–1971

CAREER STATS

FIRST TEAM ALL-STAR	6
ART ROSS TROPHY	1
CONN SMYTHE TROPHY	1
HART MEMORIAL TROPHY	2
NHL LIFETIME ACHIEVEMENT AWARD	1
NHL ALL-STAR GAME	13

STANLEY CUPS	GOALS	ASSISTS
10	507	712

BORN	AUGUST 31, 1931
NATIONALITY	CANADIAN
POSITION(S)	CENTRE
SHOT	LEFT
RETIRED	1971

Nobody in the history of the NHL has more Stanley Cups to their name. Jean Béliveau won it ten times as a player and then seven more as an executive. He did it all with his beloved Canadiens, where he broke scoring records and reinvented the way people thought bigger centers should play.

Born in Trois-Rivières on August 31, 1931, Jean Béliveau had an unsettled childhood. His father was an electrician who installed power lines, meaning the family moved a lot. Still, wherever they lived, his father always tried to build a mini rink for the kids.

It was on these homemade rinks that Jean learned his skills, and he didn't play proper hockey until he was 12. His whole education in the sport came in his backyard up until that point! Once he started playing organized hockey, he really took off.

He played for his school's team before moving on to the Victoriaville Tigres, a local college team. He spent a couple of years with the Tigres before joining the Quebec Citadelles, a minor hockey team in the AHL.

Jean spent his summers playing baseball, and his parents turned down several contract offers from top franchises when he was a teenager. Jean loved hockey, and his parents encouraged him to hold out for his dream move to the NHL, which didn't take long. Jean was spotted by Frank Selke, the Canadiens manager, when he was just 15.

Jean signed a sort of pre-contract with the Canadiens that pretty much meant they would have the first option on him if he went pro. He was playing amateur hockey at the time in the Quebec Senior Hockey League (QSHL), and he was contracted for another few years. At the time, amateur players couldn't play in the NHL, but the Canadiens wanted him as soon as possible. To make the move happen, the Canadiens' owner bought the QSHL and made it a semipro league, meaning Jean could move straight away!

Even though Jean topped out at 6-foot-3 and 205 pounds, he was known for his speed, puck-handling, grace, and agility. He changed how people thought centers should look and turned the game into a much more beautiful experience. The era of brutish, barreling players was changing, and the new breed brought elegance to the sport.

Jean became a Canadiens regular by the 1953–54 season, just as their dynasty was beginning. He played alongside other future Hall of Famers such as Maurice and Henri Richard and Doug Harvey. It was also the period of that amazing Canadiens-Red Wings rivalry when Jean and his teammates constantly battled with Gordie Howe, Glenn Hall, and the rest of those Red Wings legends.

One of those epic battles in the 1956 Stanley Cup Finals sparked the Canadiens' now-famous five in a row. Jean was a massive part of that run, and he was also crucial when they dominated again five years after it. Between 1965 and 1971, the Canadiens won the Stanley Cup five more times.

That 1965 Stanley Cup success saw Jean with the first-ever Conn Smythe Trophy.

Throughout all of this, Jean scored regularly. He was a favorite of the Canadiens fans, which was hard to do given the number of superstars on the roster. His long career with the Canadiens came to an end after that 1971 Stanley Cup victory, and he retired as the franchise's all-time leading goal scorer. It wasn't until fellow legend Guy Lafleur came along that his record was beaten. He is still second on the list today.

Along with his 10 Stanley Cups, his time with the Canadiens saw Jean register 507 goals and 712 assists (1,219 points) in 1,219 regular season games. He added 79 goals and 97 assists (162 points) in playoff games to that tally. The Canadiens retired his number 4 jersey following his retirement, and he moved upstairs and into an executive role soon after.

In his role as executive, he oversaw seven more Stanley Cup wins, putting him top of the all-time list with an unbelievable 17! Along with his Conn Smythe Trophy, Jean also won the Hart Trophy twice and the Art Ross once.

Outside of hockey, he set up the Society for Disabled Children, which has helped many kids live a better life. He passed away in 2014, much to the sadness of not only every Canadiens fan but every fan of hockey, but his name will be forever etched in the history of the Canadiens, and his 17 Stanley Cups will surely never be equaled.

RAY BOURQUE

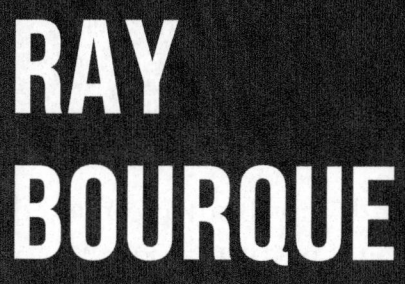

BUBBA

TEAMS

BOSTON BRUINS

1979–1999

COLORADO AVALANCHE
1999–2001

STANLEY CUPS
1

CAREER STATS

NHL FIRST TEAM ALL-STAR	13
CALDER MEMORIAL TROPHY	1
JAMES NORRIS MEMORIAL TROPHY	5
KING CLANCY MEMORIAL TROPHY	1
LESTER PATRICK TROPHY	1

GOALS	ASSISTS
410	1169

BIOGRAPHY

BORN	DECEMBER 28, 1960
NATIONALITY	CANADIAN
POSITION(S)	DEFENCE
SHOT	LEFT
RETIRED	2001

A true Boston Bruins legend, Ray Bourque played for his beloved team for 21 years, becoming known as the only defenseman who might just rival Bobby Orr in terms of attacking skill. He is the Bruins' longest-serving captain, and his loyalty to the team is something that can never be questioned. Ray won the James Norris Memorial Trophy five times and came second in the Hart Memorial voting twice, which is almost unheard of for a defenseman.

Oh, and he scored and assisted more than Bobby Orr did, which is possibly Ray Bourque's biggest achievement. Of course, Bobby stopped playing at 31, but this is still an amazing stat.

Ray was born in Saint-Laurent, Quebec, on December 28, 1960. He was raised bilingual*, and his parents spoke both French and English in the home. When Ray was just 12, he lost his mother to cancer, which affected him greatly, and he buried himself even deeper into hockey to cope.

He played nonstop as a kid, and like Nicklas Lidstrom and Jean Béliveau, he was graceful on the ice despite being a big lad. It was a talent he never lost.

Ray's talents were evident early on, but it didn't stop his first team in the Quebec Major Junior Hockey League, the Trois-Rivières Draveurs, trading him halfway through his rookie season. Ray was heartbroken at what he felt was a betrayal, so he set his mind to killing it with his new team. His positive attitude paid off, and he was named the league's best defenseman in 1978 and '79.

Although many NHL franchises looked at him before the draft, he wasn't as sought-after as some other players on this list. He was drafted eighth overall by the Bruins, who had wanted another defenseman, Keith Brown. The Bruins "settled" on Ray, much like the Islanders did with Mike Bossy a few years earlier. Both of these "gambles" turned out to be the best decisions those two franchises ever made!

Much like Ray's disappointment of being traded in his rookie season in the QMJHL, he used the lack of interest in him during the draft to spur him on. His rookie season in the NHL was fantastic, and it was kickstarted when he scored on his debut against the Winnipeg Jets. Ray ended the season with the Calder Memorial Trophy and earned a First Team All-Star selection, becoming the first non-goaltender to do so in their rookie season.

Also, there was the small matter of his 65 points, which was a record for a rookie defenseman!

Ray had joined a franchise that was getting a name as chokers. Between 1968 and 1996, the Boston Bruins made the playoffs a record 29 consecutive times! A great achievement, yes, but it came with a downside. They didn't win the Stanley Cup in any of those seasons. Of course, this was during the domination of the Canadiens first and then the Oilers. Still, it must have been tough for the fans!

Ray did taste victory with Canada, winning the Canada Cup in 1984 and then again in 1987, but Stanley Cup glory continued to evade him.

He was named co-captain in 1985 alongside Rick Middleton, with Rick captaining the team for home games while Ray would take charge when the team was on the road. When Middleton retired in 1988, Ray was named full-time captain. By the time he retired, Ray had surpassed Boston legend Dit Clapper as the longest-serving Bruins captain and Alex Delvecchio as the longest-serving NHL captain. This second record was broken by Steve Yzerman years later.

Even with the Bruins of that era struggling to win the Stanley Cup, they entertained everyone who watched them. They had a way of transitioning from defense to offense in the blink of an eye, which was mostly down to Ray's talents. In fact, the Bruins became so dependent on him that whenever he was injured (which wasn't often), the team usually lost.

Ray did reach the Stanley Cup Finals in 1988 and again in 1990, but the Bruins came up against Wayne Gretzky, Mark Messier, and that unstoppable Oilers team in each series. They lost both Finals, which really hurt Ray. He was starting to feel like he would never win the big one.

By the 1999–2000 season, nothing had changed at the Bruins. Every time it looked like they would mount a real challenge, something would go wrong. When Ray asked for a trade, the fans and his teammates understood. He needed to win the Stanley Cup, and it wasn't going to happen in Boston.

He got his move, and the Colorado Avalanche signed him in time for the 1999–2000 season. He was joining a team with the likes of Patrick Roy on the roster, so Ray felt he had a real chance of winning. In the end, he only spent one and a half seasons with the Avalanche, but he did win that Stanley Cup he dreamed of for so long.

It happened after an epic series against the New Jersey Devils, with Ray scoring the game-winning goal in Game 3. The series went to the wire, but the Avalanche won out with a 4–3 victory. Ray Bourque had waited longer than any Cup-winning player to get his hands on the trophy in the 108-year history of the Stanley Cup!

It was made even more special when, three days later, on his return to Boston with the Cup, 20,000 people lined the streets to cheer him on. The Bruins fans didn't feel bitter that he had left them to win. They understood, and they loved him for the 21 years he spent trying to win it with them.

Ray Bourque retired after that Stanley Cup success as the defenseman with the most goals and assists in the history of the NHL. He is the only defenseman that can be compared with Bobby Orr, and the Boston fans would probably see it the other way around!

WAYNE GRETZKY

THE GREAT ONE

TEAMS

INDIANAPOLIS RACERS
1978-1979

↓

EDMONTON OILERS
1979-1988

↓

LOS ANGELES KINGS
1988-1995

↓

ST. LOUIS BLUES
1995-1996

↓

NEW YORK RANGERS
1996-1999

STANLEY CUPS
4

CAREER STATS

ART ROSS TROPHY	10
CONN SMYTHE TROPHY	2
HART MEMORIAL TROPHY	9
LADY BYNG MEMORIAL TROPHY	5
LESTER PATRICK TROPHY	1
TED LINDSAY AWARD	5

GOALS	ASSISTS
894	1963

BIOGRAPHY

BORN	JANUARY 26, 1961
NATIONALITY	CANADIAN
POSITION(S)	CENTRE
SHOT	LEFT
RETIRED	1999

This list isn't numbered because it is impossible to separate so many legends. If we did number it, it's fair to say that most people would have The Great One at the top. We have put him last because his name pops up so much throughout, which only happens because he was so good that everyone else has to be compared to him! In fact, when Wayne Gretzky retired in 1999, he held 61 NHL records!

Wayne Gretzky helped reinvent the way centers played the game. Like Jean Béliveau, he proved that greediness wasn't essential to be a top scorer. Wayne was an all-round player, which is proven by the number of assists he registered throughout his career. One of his most impressive records is that he had more assists than anyone else in the NHL has registered in total points!

Where Wayne differs from Jean Béliveau is that he was smaller. And where he differed from everyone who has ever picked up a stick is how he read the game. He saw things nobody else did, and it often seemed like he was able to predict how plays would unfold even when they were happening behind him. He remained unpredictable up until the day he retired, which meant defenders couldn't figure him out.

Wayne Gretzky was born on January 26, 1961, in Brantford, Ontario. His father, Walter, was obsessed with hockey and was one of the parents who built a mini rink in the backyard for his kids to practice. In fact, when the family moved in Wayne's youth, his father picked a house with a flat yard so the rink would be perfect!

Young Wayne was a prodigy* from the moment he could walk. He was able to skate before he turned three, and by the time he was six, he was playing on a team of ten-year-olds. Even then, he was the best player on the ice, basing his game on his idol, Gordie Howe. He was so small that the jerseys were far too big for him, so he had to tuck his in on one side. It was a habit he continued throughout his NHL career.

When Wayne was 10, he had a season in the Quebec International Pee-Wee Hockey Tournament when he recorded 378 goals and 139 assists with the Brantford Nadrofsky Steelers. By 13, he had over 1,000 goals in the league, and he was so good that jealous parents often booed him from the bleachers.

Fearing for their child's mental health, Wayne's parents agreed to let him move to Toronto. This was done partly to further his career but also to get him away from the negativity of the other parents. Once in Toronto, Wayne found an even higher level.

When he was just 17, the World Hockey Association (WHA) came calling. This was in 1978, five years into the league, and it was on the verge of collapse. Still, the Indianapolis Racers believed that signing the hottest prospect in the history of the sport would save the league. They got their wish, signing Wayne on a seven-year contract, but it didn't last.

After just eight games, the Racers folded, and so did the WHA. What Wayne's signing did was force the NHL to reconsider letting some of the WHA franchises into the league. Young stars such as Wayne would come with the merger, so they agreed to let the Hartford Whalers, the Edmonton Oilers, the Winnipeg Jets, and the Quebec Nordiques become part of the NHL. This became known as the 1979 expansion.

One bit of joy Wayne did get out of that short season in the WHA was that he was selected for the league's final All-Star Games, where he got to line up alongside his hero Gordie Howe and Gordie's son Mark. The dream front line combined for seven points in Game 1!

With the first season of the Expansion Era beginning, Wayne had to choose between the Winnipeg Jets and the Edmonton Oilers as his new team. He picked the Oilers, and both his and the franchise's fortunes changed forever.

In his first season in the NHL, Wayne won the Hart Memorial Trophy, which he would go on to win for the next seven seasons in a row! He also finished tied for the Art Ross Trophy but lost out to Marcel Dionne due to his goals-assist ratio. Wayne didn't make the same mistake again and won the Art Ross in the following six seasons!

The 1981–82 season saw him score 50 goals in the first 39 games, with the last 5 coming in a single game against the Philadelphia Flyers! Later in the season, he broke Phil Esposito's record for goals in a season (76) before finally finishing with 92. He added 120 assists for a total of 212 points in 80 games, becoming the only player to surpass 200 points!

He finished the year by being named the 1982 Sportsman of the Year by Sports Illustrated, and he became the first hockey player and first Canadian to be named Associated Press Male Athlete of the Year. Wayne Gretzky was becoming world news and a genuine global superstar.

Within four years of being in the NHL, the Oilers were challenging for the Stanley Cup. They were a young, exciting, strong team with future Hall of Famers such as Mark Messier, Jari Kurri, Glenn Anderson, Paul Coffey, and Grant Fuhr on the roster. With Wayne scoring freely in attack, they were pretty unstoppable.

Wayne was named captain in 1983, and in his first year leading the team, they reached the Stanley Cup Finals. Unfortunately, they were swept by the New York Islanders, but the team used the pain to come back stronger the following year. And they did, reaching the Finals again to face the Islanders once more. This time, the Oilers won, and the franchise and Wayne had their first Stanley Cup!

Over the next five years, they would win it three more times, and then the biggest shock in NHL history would break up the party!

Wayne Gretzky was traded to the Los Angeles Kings soon after the Oilers won the 1988 Stanley Cup. It was such a shock that it is simply known as "The Trade." At first, Wayne was devastated, but later discovered that Oilers' owner Peter Pocklington's other businesses were losing money, and he wanted to cash in on his star player. Wayne agreed that he would move, but only if teammates Marty McSorley and Mike Krushelnyski were part of the trade.

A deal was agreed, and Gretzky, McSorley, and Krushelnyski moved to the Kings, with Jimmy Carson, Martin Gelinas, and $15 million going the other way.

Wayne's time at the Kings was a disaster, with only a couple of bright moments. One of them was when the Kings came up against the Oilers in his first season in LA. They met in the Smythe Division semifinals, and Wayne worried that the Edmonton fans would boo him. He couldn't have been more wrong, and they cheered him throughout, even when the Kings won.

The 1993–94 season saw him surpass Gordie Howe's goal-scoring record, but things never really worked out in LA. Wayne asked for a trade in 1996, and he moved to the St. Louis Blues before joining up with former teammate Mark Messier at the New York Rangers.

Wayne Gretzky retired in 1999, and even though he played for four different franchises in the NHL, he will always be remembered for his time with the Oilers. Most of his records still stand, and it is hard to imagine a lot of them ever being broken. His list of personal honors would take up this whole book, so let's just agree that there has never been anyone like The Great One in any sport!

AT THE BUZZER

We hope you had a good time learning about some of these legends of the NHL, and we hope we didn't miss any of your favorites. Of course, there will be players who didn't make the list that you might feel should have, but that's the beauty of sports. We get to have our own opinions.

As you will have seen, some of the players on this list had to come through some pretty hard times. Can you imagine trying to play as World War II raged? Or how about those guys who worked on farms as kids while having to go to school in between? Life can be tough sometimes, but as these players have shown, there is always a light at the end of the tunnel if you give your all.

The NHL continues to be the most-watched hockey league in the world, and it always delivers on action, drama, and passion. Every year, the competition seems to grow fiercer, and that's why we love to tune in. One of the best parts about watching is that we might be seeing a new legend being created right before our eyes when a rookie scores a goal or blocks a shot.

We can each think, Have I just seen the new Mark Messier or Bobby Hull?

And when we see these guys in action, doesn't it make

us believe we can achieve anything? If Mike Bossy and Bobby Orr can come through their tough childhoods to be stars of the NHL, then anything is possible! We just have to believe.

And as our time together comes to an end, and the buzzer is about to sound, we hope that you enjoyed your time learning about some of the most legendary players in the NHL. Even if hockey isn't your favorite sport, there is something to be learned from these guys. It takes immense skill and dedication to reach the top in any walk of life, and hockey is no different. Only the best of the best get to step out onto that ice.

So, have you been able to decide who is the greatest? It's not easy, is it? Maybe you can break it down into sections: Best Goaltender, Best Defenseman, Best Winger, and Best Center. Even then, it's still pretty hard to separate them!

Either way, we hope you have fun trying!

GLOSSARY

Affiliate - A team or business that is part of a larger team or business.

Bamboozle - To do something unexpected that confuses.

Bankruptcy - When a person or business is legally unable to pay their bills, they can declare bankruptcy and have some or all of their debt forgiven.

Bilingual - Can speak two different languages.

Champing at the bit - Very eager and excited to get started.

Consecutive - In a row.

Czechoslovakia - A country before it split into the Czech Republic and Slovakia on December 31, 1992.

Durable - Able to withstand a lot of pressure or damage.

Expansion Era - This started when six new franchises were added to the league in 1967 and continued until 1992, although some people would claim it stopped in 1978 when the WHA folded.

Fever Pitch - Extreme excitement.

Hierarchy - The more powerful people in an organization or country.

Hodgkin's disease - A form of cancer.

Hurling - A stick-and-ball sport that originated in Ireland and can be traced back more than 3,000 years! It is still played in Ireland today.

Inaugural - The start or first of something.

Longevity - Able to last.

Lucrative - A lot of money.

Machinist - Someone who works using a machine, like a printing press or sewing machine.

Malnourished - Weak and ill due to lack of food.

Merged - Joined together.

Milestone - An important stage or event in time.

Neurological disease - A disease that affects the brain or spinal cord.

Nine official dynasties in NHL history - Ottawa Senators (1919–1927), Toronto Maple Leafs (1946–1951), Detroit Red Wings (1949–1955), Montreal Canadiens (1955–1960), Toronto Maple Leafs (1961–1967), Montreal Canadiens (1964–1969), Montreal Canadiens (1975–1979), New York Islanders (1979–1983), Edmonton Oilers (1983–1990).

Original Six - The six teams that made up the NHL between 1942 and 1967 (Boston Bruins, Chicago Blackhawks, Montreal Canadiens, Toronto Maple Leafs, Detroit Red Wings, and New York Rangers).

Prodigy - A child who is exceptional at something.

Radiation treatment - A painful treatment that tries to kill cancer cells.

Turmoil - Not in a good state.

Wane - To become weaker.

World Hockey Association - Operated in North America between 1972 and 1979 as a competitor to the National Hockey League.

Printed in Great Britain
by Amazon

37679671R00069